the private nuclear strategists

Roy E. Licklider

the private
nuclear strategists

Ohio State University Press

To my mother,
who by act, example, and inspiration
made all things possible

acknowledgments

Major intellectual contributions to this study were made by Robert Axelrod, Karl W. Deutsch, Harold D. Lasswell, J. David Singer, and H. Bradford Westerfield. I received generous financial support from the Council on International Relations, Yale University; National Science Foundation Grant No. 2635 to the World Data Analysis Program, Yale University; and supplemental computer funds from NSF. In addition to these I have contracted many other debts. The staff of the Yale Computer Center bore with my constant state of crisis. Philip J. Stone made the Harvard computer facilities available to me. Duncan MacRae provided an important computer program. Morton H. Halperin, William W. Kaufmann, and Fred C. Ikle allowed me to pretest my questionnaire on their Harvard and M.I.T. classes, and about twenty of their graduate students were good enough to cooperate. Among the many libraries whose facilities I used, the excellent collection of the New York Peace Information Center should be singled out. Finally, my wife Patricia braved my writing style and read proofs with me.

But my primary debts are two, one individual and one collective. Bruce Russett was a model dissertation director. He posed alternatives, gave authoritative advice, and accepted my decisions even when he disagreed with them. Despite his other commitments, he always made himself available when wanted. In the end, however, the study hinged on the cooperation of 191 respondents, most of whom I have never met. I owe them heartfelt thanks, and I hope the result was worth their effort.

R.E.L.

September, 1971

contents

list of tables

the private nuclear strategists

chapter one

introduction

It has become a cliché that the combination of nuclear weapons and clashing nationalisms poses the single most important challenge of our time. A failure in this field could make all other problems irrelevant by destroying civilization as we know it, if not the human race itself. Given the significance of the problem, the nature of the people who deal with it is of considerable interest.

Borrowing a term from Wesley Posvar,[1] and somewhat expanding its original meaning, we define the *strategic community* as those individuals concerned with organized violence in the international arena. Before World War II it was clearly defined. In a convenient reflection of the supposed American dichotomy of peace and war, foreign policy was divided between the diplomats and the military. Thus the pre–World War II strategic

1. Wesley W. Posvar, "Strategy Expertise and National Security," Ph.D. dissertation (Harvard University, April, 1964), p. 2.

community was essentially made up of the professional military. It is true that it also included a group of civil servants who worked in the War and Navy Departments, but these regarded themselves as instruments of the military and were concerned with service functions rather than strategy. The notable exception to this, of course, was the president, who is constitutionally both a civilian and commander in chief of the armed forces;[2] depending on the personalities involved, the civilian secretaries of war and the navy were sometimes also directly involved in strategy. Nevertheless, strategy was generally left to the professional soldier; indeed, it was a subject of real public interest only during and immediately preceding wartime, with the exception of the neo-Hamiltonianism of Alfred Mahan and Leonard Wood, and even here the seminal writing was done by military men. Although subject to occasional challenge, the soldier was recognized as *the* professional expert in military strategy.[3]

The institution of total war, however, changed this situation somewhat; at a minimum the military was forced to call upon civilian experts for assistance in sectors of the war effort that it was ill-prepared to control. Problems of a war economy, for instance, gave rise to a long struggle for control by the military and civilians. World War II especially saw the introduction of physical and social scientists into the war effort. Physical scientists were concerned with developing new tools of war; the variable time fuse, radar, and jet aircraft were prominent examples, overshadowed by the Manhattan Project, which produced the

2. For historical case studies of this dual role, see Ernest R. May, ed., *The Ultimate Decision: The President as Commander in Chief* (New York: George Braziller, 1960).

3. For detailed discussions of these questions, see, *inter alia*, Samuel P. Huntington, *The Soldier and the State: The Theory and Politics of Civil-Military Relations* (Cambridge, Mass.: Harvard University Press, Belknap Press, 1959), pp. 143–312; Paul Y. Hammond, *Organizing for Defense: The American Military Establishment in the Twentieth Century* (Princeton, N.J.: Princeton University Press, 1964), pp. 1–106; Louis Smith, *American Democracy and Military Power* (Chicago: University of Chicago Press, 1951), pp. 102–51.

first atomic bomb. Social scientists were also involved, many for the first time, in national defense. They tested American servicemen, produced propaganda, studied the effects of bombing, and advised the military during campaigns in little-known areas of the world, especially in Asia.

However, most of this effort by civilians during the war was under government sponsorship and was not concerned with strategy; the scientists were helping to wage war more effectively, not suggesting how it should be done. The one major effort to do just this, the Franck memorandum from some members of the Manhattan Project on the use of the atomic bomb, was a notable failure.[4] The end of the war saw the return of most of these individuals to their normal jobs, but many had been deeply affected by their experience.

It is worth noting that a somewhat similar pattern of activity had marked World War I as well, although on a smaller scale. The work during World War I, however, seemed to produce little or no carryover into the postwar years; but the post–World War II years involved a major shift in membership in the strategic community. This was due to at least three factors: (1) the nation was still faced with a major long-term security problem after World War II; (2) the atomic scientists especially felt a personal responsibility for the atomic bomb and were deeply concerned about its future; and (3) operations research had developed a set of methods that could be applied to some aspects of strategy.

Depending on the viewpoint, the United States faced either or both of two major threats to its national security involving military strategy: Russian imperialism and the atomic bomb. This was in sharp contrast to the situation after World War I, when the biggest external menace the United States could find was the Royal Navy. Given this situation, the government took steps to ensure that at least some of the scientists who had been

---

4. Michael Amrine, *The Great Decision: The Secret History of the Atomic Bomb* (New York: G. P. Putnam's Sons, 1959), pp. 96–111, 142–49, 182–83.

involved in defense work during the war remained available, such as the establishment of the national laboratory system.

A very different motivation brought other people into the arena. The destruction of Hiroshima and Nagasaki, together with the threat that nuclear weapons posed to the world, and the seeming inability of political leaders to cope with it produced a movement among some of the scientists who had been involved in the Manhattan Project, and who felt largely responsible for the atomic bomb, to educate the public and to explore ways whereby atomic energy might never again be used in war. One early product of the movement was the establishment of the *Bulletin of the Atomic Scientists,* which continues to be an influential publication in the field. Although the atomic scientists supplied much of the initial impetus and gave the movement a name, they were willing to include other physical and social scientists. Most of the people in this movement were outside of government and remained so; they found themselves a vocal, although not always coherent, group putting forth alternate military strategies to those of the administration.[5] An unintentional by-product of this movement was a reaction among other physical scientists, mobilizing those who supported the administration's policies.

During World War II the techniques of operations research were developed and applied to military problems with some success by physical scientists and mathematicians. At this time it was used on tactical rather than strategic problems, but its utility was great enough to justify the establishment of a series of nonprofit research corporations under government contract, of which the RAND Corporation was both the first and the best known.[6] Later during the postwar years, and largely at these

5. For extensive discussion of this movement, see Robert G. Gilpin, *American Scientists and Nuclear Weapons* (Princeton, N.J.: Princeton University Press, 1962) and Alice Kimball Smith, *A Peril and a Hope: The Scientists' Movement in America, 1945–1947* (Chicago: University of Chicago Press, 1965).

6. See Bruce L. R. Smith, *The RAND Corporation: Case Study of a Non-Profit Research Institute* (Cambridge, Mass.: Harvard University Press, 1966).

institutions, operations research was broadened to systems analysis and applied to the larger problems of strategy. In order to tap the minds of those individuals who did not want to leave their university teaching positions, research centers were established at many schools throughout the nation. These organizations grew and proliferated, and their members became in part intellectual competitors with the military within the strategic community. Since many of the personnel in both the scientists' movement and the research corporations came from academic life, it is not surprising that there was some feedback; courses were introduced at some universities on strategy and disarmament at both the graduate and undergraduate level.[7]

The result is that the strategic community has been considerably enlarged beyond the professional military, and after twenty years there is no indication that the change is a transient one. It is difficult to contend that either the military or civilians have been dominant in strategic decisions; it varies with the individual decision, and in any case the lines of debate within the strategic community tend to cut across rather than to reinforce the military-civilian division.[8]

Our knowledge about the inner workings of the strategic community is rather scanty considering its significance. We may, for the sake of convenience, divide it into three different groups: the professional military, civilians employed by the government (public civilian strategists), and civilians outside of government (private civilian strategists). The professional military has been the subject of at least one major recent study;[9] indeed, military sociology has become a semi-recognized subfield in sociology, although this is deceptive since much of the work under this

7. The best intellectual history of this process is Gene M. Lyons and Louis Morton, *Schools for Strategy: Education and Research in National Security Affairs* (New York: Frederick A. Praeger, Publishers, 1965).

8. Gene M. Lyons, "The New Civil-Military Relations," *American Political Science Review* 55(1961), 53–63; Smith, *RAND Corporation*, pp. 20–39.

9. Morris Janowitz, *The Professional Soldier: A Social and Political Portrait* (New York: Free Press of Glencoe, Inc., 1960).

rubric is concerned with psychological testing of military personnel. We know relatively little about civilians employed by the government, although there is some evidence available on their policy perspectives.[10]

The third group, civilians outside of government, has attracted considerable popular attention in the past few years, but we know very little about it. They have written most of the new extensive literature on strategy and disarmament since World War II; the new language and terminology of deterrence is largely a product of their work. Working under fewer inhibitions because they are more free of government responsibilities, they have conducted a public strategic debate over the past ten years that has significantly raised the general level of public information and debate and that has at least accompanied, if it is not the sole cause of, major changes in strategy by the American government. Some of its members have been influential in formulating American foreign and military policy, both as government officials (there is some mobility between this group and those employed by government) and advisers; others have led vocal opposition to the same policies.

There is a small but growing literature on the relationship of this group with government and policy. There are two major studies of the policy positions of individual group members, indicating the wide diversity of such views.[11] There is also some harsh criticism of the group, again representative of a broad spectrum

---

10. Lloyd Jensen, "American Foreign Policy Elites and the Prediction of International Events," *Papers* of the Peace Research Society (International), 5 (1966), 199–209. For a comparison of military officers and foreign service officers, see Bernard Mennis, *American Foreign Policy Officials; Who They Are and What They Believe* (Columbus: Ohio State University Press, 1971).

11. Robert A. Levine, *The Arms Debate* (Cambridge, Mass.: Harvard University Press, 1963); Arthur Herzog, *The War-Peace Establishment* (New York: Harper & Row, 1965). The latter is rather journalistic in style but still useful.

of opinion.[12] A recent contribution has been an intellectual history of the group.[13] There are also two doctoral dissertations that should be mentioned, the first by a sympathetic member of the professional military, the second focusing on the role of social scientists in the area.[14]

Although these works differ widely in quality, sophistication, and motivation, they share an impressionistic approach. Indeed, we know remarkably little about the individuals who make up this group. We know that they come from many different backgrounds and academic disciplines; various authors have noted the influence of physical scientists and economists, among others. But we do not know what percentage is from each discipline or what difference it makes to their theoretical and policy orientations.[15] It is obvious that there are many subgroups within the field, but we have no real knowledge about their size, location, or significance. We know that members of the group are employed by industrial corporations, research institutes, universities, and

12. See, e.g., General Thomas D. White, "Strategy and the Defense Intellectuals," *Saturday Evening Post*, 236 (May 4, 1963), pp. 10–12; Irving Horowitz, *The War Game: Studies of the New Civilian Militarists* (New York: Ballantine Books, Inc., 1963); Philip Green, *Deadly Logic: The Theory of Nuclear Deterrence* (Columbus: Ohio State University Press, 1966); Anatol Rapoport, *Strategy and Conscience* (New York: Harper & Row, 1964); Saul Friedman, "The RAND Corporation and Our Policy Makers," *Atlantic Monthly* 212 (1963), 61–68; H. L. Nieburg, *In the Name of Science* (Chicago: Quadrangle Books, 1966).

13. Lyons and Morton, *Schools for Strategy.*

14. Posvar, "Strategy Expertise and National Security"; and *Social Conflict* (tentative title) by Kathleen Archibald, to be published by Basic Books, Inc., Publishers, New York. Permission to reprint granted by the Publishers. (All page references are to manuscript.)

15. For interesting speculation on this subject, see Lyons and Morton, *Schools for Strategy*, pp. 51–98; Warner R. Schilling, "Scientists, Foreign Policy, and Politics," Albert Wohlstetter, "Strategy and the Natural Scientists," and Bernard Brodie, "The Scientific Strategists," in Robert Gilpin and Christopher Wright, eds., *Scientists and National Policy-Making* (New York: Columbia University Press, 1964), pp. 144–73, 174–239, 240–56; Bernard Brodie, "The McNamara Phenomenon," *World Politics* 17 (1965), 679.

the federal government; but there is no data on proportions in these institutions, mobility between them, or whether each tends to hire different types of people. We have nothing but informed speculation about why group members decided to enter the field. This study is designed to correct this lack of information, at least in part.

population and sample

The subject of this study is one part of the strategic community: those individuals who are concerned with nuclear strategy and disarmament and who are not employed by the government. Neither limitation is as easy to define in practice as it might appear. This group was chosen, however, for three major reasons:

1. It is the single most important field within the strategic community because of the magnitude of the stakes involved.

2. Civilians outside of government have clearly been influential in the area, partially because of the relative novelty of the topic. Not only have they furnished most of the vocabulary and conceptualization, but they have practically invented the whole idea of arms control that has become a recognized part of American policy.

3. It is a distinctive field; nuclear strategy and disarmament is not closely related to other areas of study, and it is relatively simple to determine when an individual is working in the area.

Nuclear strategy and disarmament is a term capable of varied interpretation; for purposes of the study it was defined as *nuclear weapons policy*. It thus excluded such subjects as civil-military relations, cost-effectiveness, government organization, military assistance, the economics of disarmament, counterinsurgency, military history, operations research, simulation, civil defense, intelligence, and much of the material labeled peace research or conflict theory, unless work in these areas was directly and explicitly linked to nuclear weapons policy.

The question of what constitutes employment by the government can also become complex; in practice it was defined quite strictly to *exclude* only those who were working full time directly for the federal government. Individuals who did part-time consulting work were *included*, as were those who worked for organizations under government contract, such as the RAND Corporation. The problems of individuals who have moved into and out of government will be discussed below.

With these two limitations spelled out, a criterion was sought to operationalize the term *private nuclear strategist*. Several criteria were suggested. Attendance at conferences on the topic was one possiblity. A list of government researchers might have been obtained. Well-known individuals in the field could be asked for names. Organizations might have been regarded as the unit of analysis rather than individuals; individuals could then be selected from among their employees. Mailing lists of individuals and/or organizations might have been useful. A journal could have been approached and asked to cooperate by making its subscription list available.

All of these ideas, however, seemed more appropriate to a field whose boundaries were fairly well established. A recent study of political scientists, for instance, used membership in the American Political Science Association as its criterion for establishing a population.[16] However, the area of interest discussed here is not well defined. There seemed to be no journal or organization that linked people working in nuclear strategy and disarmament (nor did one turn up during the course of the study); and it was known that members came into the area from a variety of backgrounds and held very different policy views. It was

16. Albert Somit and Joseph Tanenhaus, *American Political Science: A Profile of a Discipline* (New York: Atherton Press, 1964), pp. 13 n., 140–41.

decided, therefore, to concentrate on the public strategic debate because of an interest in communication flows within the group and because this method seemed the most likely to include a large number of very different people whose only common link appeared to be an interest in a particular subject area. Specifically, any individual was included if he had written, in the nineteen years between the beginning of 1946 and the end of 1964 (the first postwar year up to the year before the study was begun) concerning nuclear weapons policy:

1. one or more books, or
2. three or more
   a. articles in books
   b. articles in periodicals included in one of several major periodical indexes
   c. papers reproduced and circulated by any of a large number of formal organizations or institutes
   d. papers at a professional conference that dealt primarily with nuclear weapons policy

Perhaps the major weakness of this criterion was that classified literature could not be included, since there was no access to the lists of such material. It is unclear how many individuals were excluded from the study because of this limitation. One respondent suggested that the classified literature was at least as large as the unclassified, but there is a good deal of overlap between the authors of the two literatures; certainly, many of those who have done classified work are in the population. However, there are some individuals who do no public work whatsoever, and they may well have considerable impact upon government policies.

One problem was the classification of a substantial number of individuals who worked for the government and later returned to private life. Those who had written about nuclear strategy and disarmament only when they were in government were to be excluded from the study; on the other hand, if an individual had written in the field while he was not in government, his current status would be logically irrelevant. Therefore, the cutting point for government employment was set as the time when a book or article was published, not to the individual's current status. For example, Raymond Garthoff wrote extensively in the field while a private citizen; the fact that he is now employed by the government did not exclude him from the population. By the same token, retired military personnel who had written in the field after leaving the armed forces were included.

In order to establish the population, a master bibliography of approximately 6,000 file cards was compiled on writings on nuclear weapons policy from the beginning of 1946 through 1964. This in turn was the product of 93 published bibliographies, 4 periodical indexes, the unclassified sections of the Armed Services Technical Information Agency's *Technical Abstract Bulletin,* over 250 letters requesting publication lists from various organizations, and miscellaneous other sources.[17] This process yielded a population of 491 individuals. The principal research instrument was a mail questionnaire.[18] Since it was to be sent to all members of the population, pre-testing presented something of a problem. With the generous assistance of Professors Morton H. Halperin, Fred C. Ikle, and William W. Kaufmann, copies of the first draft of the questionnaire were circulated to graduate students at Harvard and M.I.T. taking courses in strategy and disarmament. As a result of this pre-testing, several changes were made in the questionnaire. Copies of the final draft were sent to all members of the population on May 23, 1966. Follow-up letters and questionnaires were sent to those who had not replied in July and again in September of the same year.

Of the 491 members of the population, 191 returned their questionnaires; these 191 make up the sample. The return rate

17. Detailed information may be found in Appendix A.
18. Appendix B contains a copy of the mail questionnaire.

was 39 percent, a reasonably high figure considering that the questionnaire was an intimidating eleven pages long and that it was connected with a doctoral dissertation, which made the publication of its results problematical. The questionnaires were supplemented by sixteen personal interviews with respondents, most of these during June and July, 1967, when the study was being completed. These interviews focused upon a few particular areas where questionnaire results seemed inadequate, especially morals, responsiblity, and the impact of training in a particular academic discipline. Subjects were chosen on the basis of responses to questions on these subjects included in the mail questionnaire. These two sources provided the data for this study.

One problem of any survey-based study is non-response. Although the response rate was high enough to be useful in analysis, the fact remains that over half of the population did not return their questionnaires. Therefore, an attempt was made to gather data on the non-respondents, to determine if the sample was representative of the population. The procedures and findings of this analysis are presented in Appendix C; in summary they indicate that although the sample overrepresents political scientists, it otherwise seems sufficiently representative of the population for analysis and generalization.

the lack of communities

Underlying the original concept of the study was the single hypothesis that the private nuclear strategists were divided into a few distinctive subgroups or communities. Robert Levine had already established a continuum of *policy positions*, although he carefully noted that his work was an intellectual construct rather than an actual reflection of the policy reasoning of any individual.[19] It was hypothesized that most individuals would indeed fall into one of several such policy categories, whether or not

19. Levine, *The Arms Debate*, pp. vi–vii.

Levine's particular scheme was applicable. It was further hypothesized that these divisions would be reinforced by other differences, including academic disciplines, military service, motives for working in the field, periodicals read, choice of individuals who had made a significant contribution to the area, and perhaps some insitutional or geographic affiliation. Essentially, it was hypothesized that Levine's hypothetical policy categories were existing social communities.

These expectations, in turn, were based on the tendency of many people working in the area, both in writing and private conversation, to refer to individuals as belonging to such groups. An individual might be identified, apparently with no need for further elucidation, as "one of the Pennsylvania group," a "midwestern peace researcher," a "RAND-type," an "ex-colonel," or a "peacenik." Some of this is simply in-group jargon and is not to be taken too seriously; however, it does in general seem an accurate reflection of the perceptions of many individuals working in the area. An attempt was made to discern the empirical foundations, if any, for such perceptions.

The significance of this hypothesis was shown by its corollaries. It was expected that communication would be largely *within* rather than *between* communities and that the little intercommunity communication that existed would be largely restricted to influentials. An individual with a new idea or policy suggestion would thus have to sell it separately to each different community, using its own particular periodicals, jargon, and legitimizing influentials, obviously a long and involved process. Moreover, it seemed likely that the communities would be hostile to one another; thus an individual who was identified as belonging to one community or another would have his views automatically discounted by members of other communities. Indeed, the acceptance of an idea by one community might well preclude its approval by another, regardless of its merits. Although these hypotheses followed from the original assumption of communities, they too were supported by the rhetoric of members of the population.

This whole theoretical structure was based upon the original hypothesis of communities within the population. In the event, it collapsed with it, for we were unable to substantiate the original hypothesis from our data. Although there are certainly significant differences within the sample, they do not seem to reinforce one another to create several distinct communities. This conclusion is based both on a single large-factor analysis of the data as a whole that yielded trivial results[20] and on the more particular analysis of the following chapters. There simply are no differences that cut across several sets of variables, as predicted. The data resemble the pattern called "cross-cutting cleavages," where knowledge of one particular attribute does not help predict other characteristics of different sorts. Although some people may belong to our hypothetical communities, they form at most a very small percentage of the sample.

The implications of rejecting a hypothesis are often less clear than those of its substantiation, as is the case here. It cannot be said that rejecting the hypothetical communities disproved the existence of the barriers to communication as well. All that can be said is that several major predicted barriers do not seem to exist. We will study some indicators of communications—such as periodicals read, professional organization membership, choice of influentials, and job mobility—in some detail, but no single overarching scheme emerges from this analysis to replace that which has been rejected.

---

20. The factor analysis of 244 variables yielded seven factors that together accounted for less than 25 percent of the variance. The program was the DATA-TEXT factor analysis program, using the principal components method; both varimax and quartimax rotations were used, giving essentially similar results. Professor Philip Stone generously made the facilities of the Harvard Computer Center available to me.

the perceived
influentials

Influence in the sample, as in most social groups, is not
distributed equally. The criterion of influence utilized the traditional academic approach: the judgment of an individual's colleagues. Question 34 read:

In your opinion, what individuals have made the most significant
contribution to the study of strategy and disarmament since World
War II?

The first five responses were coded (less than 5 percent of the
sample named more than this number). Disregarding responses
such as "many," "none," and "don't know," as well as eight people who named themselves, there were 536 responses.

These responses indicate that the population is something more
than merely a creation of the study. The question did not restrict
responses to the population, although the nature of the study
may have had some influence. A total of 413 responses (78 per-

cent of the total) were from members of the population.[1] Since the list of influentials is an artifact of the sample, there are two possible interpretations of this fact. If the sample is correct (if perceived influentials are actually influential), the method of selection has isolated an influential group. If the sample is incorrect, the group has a fair amount of internal cohesion, since it regards its members as being influential even when this is untrue.

It would be interesting to know which interpretation is correct. This, however, would require responses from individuals outside the population, such as government officials, and this information was not obtained. However, either interpretation suggests that the selection criterion isolated an interesting and important population.

One logical route to perceived influential status seemed to be publications. This was explored with the publication point score. Using the master bibliography, an index of publication points was established; one point was given for every article or paper published (no extra points were given for reprints, and no respondent was given more than three points for a single book), and three points were given for every book written on nuclear weapons policy. Scores ranged from 3 (the minimum required for inclusion in the population) to 50 (for Bernard Brodie). Table 1 confirms that the influentials were more likely to have high publication point scores than the rest of the sample. In fact, of the 27 individuals who had scores of over fifteen, 56 percent were perceived influentials.

It was also expected that date of birth and perceived influential status would be related, with the older groups contributing a larger percentage of influentials. Although there is some basis for this, the relationship was actually curvilinear. Again, for the sake of convenience, a variable was divided into fairly arbitrary categories: date of birth was restricted to four periods (1880–1899,

---

1. Forty (7 percent) were foreigners; 30 (6 percent) were deceased; 29 (5 percent) were civilian government officials; 23 (4 percent) were potential members of the population (that is, civilians outside of government); and only one was a military man.

Table 1

PERCEIVED INFLUENTIALS AND PUBLICATION POINTS*

Publication Points	Perceived Influentials	Others
3-5	10%	63%
6-15	53%	29%
Over 15	37%	8%
Total	100%	100%
(Number)	(40)	(150)

* Significance level: .0001. "Significance level is the probability that the relationship in question would occur by chance if there were no differences between the groups under consideration. By convention the .05, 01, and .001 levels are considered theresholds of statistical significance; however, although these are useful, they are only conventions and have no particular intrinsic significance. For the purposes of this study, significance levels of over .05 were considered significant, those between .05 and .20 notable, and those under .20 not significant (abbreviated to NS in tables). Notable relationships will normally only be discussed if they confirm patterns established by significant relationships. Unless otherwise specified, all significance level figures in this study are based on the chi square statistic. Strictly speaking, this measure is not appropriate, since there is no random sample. However, Appendix C suggests that there are few obvious distortion in the sample, and it was felt that the value of having a measure of the strength of statistical relationships justified the risks, as long as it was not interpreted too strictly.

Table 2

PERCEIVED INFLUENTIALS AND DATE OF BIRTH*

Date of Birth	Perceived Influentials	Others
1880-1899	5%	10%
1900-1919	58%	38%
1920-1939	37%	51%
1940-1959	0%	1%
Total	100%	100%
(Number)	(38)	(146)

* Significance level: .15

1900–1919, 1920–1939, and 1940–1959). Table 2 shows that the 1900–1919 group included over half of the perceived influentials, whereas the median age of the remainder of the sample was significantly lower. However, the oldest group, those born between 1880 and 1899, actually had a somewhat smaller percentage of perceived influentials than of the remainder of the sample. This may be the result of the novelty of the area. Dating the real growth of the field from the middle 1950s (the Wohlstetter bases study, which started in 1951,[2] and the publication of Henry Kissinger's *Nuclear Weapons and Foreign Policy*[3] are convenient demarcation points of the incubation period), it has been in existence ten to fifteen years. It seems likely that talented people would be more interested in entering a new area of study early in their professional careers, perhaps when they are first looking for a specialty in which to distinguish themselves. This age group would have been perhaps 30–50 years old in the middle 1950s; making allowances for the effect of World War II interrupting professional careers, this may explain the heavy concentration of influentials in this particular age group.

an academic trend?

Aside from publication points and age, the differences between the perceived influentials and the rest of the sample appear to be unimportant, in background factors, perceived influence, and

2. A. J. Wohlstetter et al., "Selection and Use of Strategic Air Bases," R-266, RAND Corporation, Santa Monica, California, April 1, 1954 (declassified, 1962), 383 pp.; for discussion of this study, see Bruce L. R. Smith, "Strategic Expertise and National Security Policy: A Case Study," *Public Policy* 13 (1964), 76–87, revised as Chapter VI, Smith, *The RAND Corporation*, pp. 195–240; E. S. Quade, "The Selection and Use of Strategic Air Bases: A Case History," and Albert Wohlstetter, "Analysis and Design of Conflict Systems," in E. S. Quade, ed., *Analysis for Military Decisions* (Chicago: Rand McNally & Co., 1964), pp. 24–63, 122–27.

3. Henry A. Kissinger, *Nuclear Weapons and Foreign Policy* (New York: Harper & Bros., 1957).

policy attitudes. In fact, the only significant division located between the two groups seems to be decreasing; this concerns the group of variables that I have labeled "academic."

There is evidence that the sample as a whole, led by the perceived influentials, is becoming more academically oriented; in the process it is reducing one potentially important difference between the influentials and the rest of the sample. This also suggests that the academic component of the peculiar intellectual-policy tension that characterizes national security policy is becoming dominant. This was by no means a foregone conclusion, given the amount of work done under government contract and the policy orientation of much of the work in the area. Moreover, the creation of the research institutes gave the policy-oriented an alternate set of institutions to the university in which to base themselves and their work.[4]

This tendency was reflected in the highest earned academic degree, the school at which it was taken, and affiliation with an academic discipline. In each instance, among the older respondents the perceived influentials were significantly more academically oriented than the remainder of the group, whereas among the younger individuals the difference was not significant because those who were not perceived influentials were more academically oriented than their older counterparts.

Since there are no Ph.D's being offered in strategic studies,[5] it is not intuitively obvious that possession of a doctoral degree is a useful indicator of the quality of an individual's work in strategy and disarmament. Nevertheless, Table 3 shows that among the older respondents the perceived influentials were significantly more likely to have this degree than the remainder of the group, and among younger respondents the non-influentials increased their percentage of doctorates to narrow the gap between them and the perceived influentials. (Indeed, the entire

4. Archibald, *Social Conflict*, chap. 3, pp. 34–39.

5. Such a program was considered by M.I.T. some years ago but was not adopted.

Table 3

PERCEIVED INFLUENTIALS, DATE OF BIRTH,
AND HIGHEST-EARNED ACADEMIC DEGREE

Degree	1900-1919*		1920-1939†	
	Perceived Influentials	Others	Perceived Influentials	Others
No college degree	4%	5%	0%	2%
Bachelor	5%	36%	7%	24%
Master	9%	20%	14%	14%
Doctorate	73%	33%	72%	49%
Legal and Medical	9%	6%	7%	8%
Total	100%	100%	100%	100%
(Number)	(22)	(55)	(14)	(73)

* **Significance level: .02**

† **Significance level: NS**

sample was remarkably well educated; 46 percent had a doctoral
degree). The American academic community, of course, has long
stressed the importance of the Ph.D.[6]

A somewhat similar situation exists in regard to the schools at
which those degrees are taken. Although it is true that a good
deal of the pioneering work in national security policy in universities was done at Harvard, Columbia, and Princeton, it was
by no means limited to those Ivy League schools.[7] However, there
was a clear relationship between the school attended and perceived influential status for the older respondents; the difference
again disappeared among the younger individuals, due to changes
by the younger non-influentials.

6. Theodore Caplow and Reece J. McGee, *The Academic Marketplace*
(New York: Science Editions, Inc., 1961), p. 162; Somit and Tanenhaus,
American Political Science, pp. 108–16.

7. Lyons and Morton, *Schools for Strategy*, pp. 127–99.

Dividing colleges and universities into categories is always ticklish. The division between state and private schools is fairly obvious, although whether it is meaningful is not so clear. Dividing the private schools, however, is a problem. I have used traditional division of Ivy League and non–Ivy League; for clarity the latter will be referred to as private schools. This gave a useful division, with about half of the sample having their highest degrees from an Ivy League school and the remainder divided about evenly between the other two categories. (Only two respondents said they took their highest degree from a military academy or school; thirteen more attended a foreign school.)

It is interesting to examine the relationship between schools, age, and perceived influentials while controlling for the field of study in which the degree was taken, as in Table 4. One would expect to find differences here if measuring influence in the parent discipline. Whereas the Ivy League universities have traditionally been regarded as superior in the social sciences and humanities, the best schools for physical science and engineering have been the private ones. In fact, the graduate school of an individual has a considerable impact upon his academic career.[8] But it is not obvious why a physical scientist from an Ivy League school or a social scientist from a private school should be less capable in strategy and disarmament, as opposed to his own discipline.[9]

Because we were working with four variables, Table 4 has some low Ns; this in turn makes statistical significance elusive. (For example, among the younger respondents in the physical sciences, all of the perceived influentials took their degrees at private schools. However, because of the small Ns, the difference was significant at only .15.) Nevertheless, the direction is clear. Among those taking degrees in physical sciences, the perceived

8. Caplow and McGee, *The Academic Marketplace*, pp. 225–26; Somit and Tanenhaus, *American Political Science*, pp. 28–48.

9. I am highly dubious about the supposed qualitative distinctions between these schools in the major disciplines as well; however, there is no gainsaying that a considerable prestige difference does exist.

Table 4

PERCEIVED INFLUENTIALS, DATE OF BIRTH, FIELD OF STUDY
OF HIGHEST-EARNED ACADEMIC DEGREE, AND SCHOOL

Field of Study and School	1900-1919*		1920-1939†	
	Perceived Influentials	Others	Perceived Influentials	Others
Physical Sciences				
Ivy League............	17%	25%	0%	23%
Private..............	33%	17%	100%	23%
State................	17%	58%	0%	31%
Military..............	0%	0%	0%	8%
Foreign.............	33%	0%	0%	15%
Total..............	100%	100%	100%	100%
(Number)	(6)	(12)	(3)	(13)
Social Sciences				
Ivy League............	64%	25%	78%	50%
Private..............	27%	44%	22%	31%
State................	0%	25%	0%	16%
Foreign.............	9%	6%	0%	3%
Total..............	100%	100%	100%	100%
(Number)	(11)	(16)	(9)	(32)

* Significance levels: physical sciences, .10; social sciences, .15

† Significance levels: physical sciences, .15; social sciences, NS

‡ No respondents took their highest degrees in the social sciences at military schools.

influentials tended to have done so at one of the private schools;
there was relatively little difference between the two age groups.
Of those who had studied in the social sciences, on the other
hand, the perceived influentials tended to have worked at the
Ivy League schools. However, this difference was greatest among

the older age group; the non-influentials among the younger group were more similar to the perceived influentials of both age groups than to their older opposite numbers.

It appears that, despite immersion in this special area, qualifications for being perceived as influential remain similar to those of the parent discipline. This could be checked by seeing if the perceived influentials were named on a similar list of their own discipline; but such lists do not appear to exist now, with one partial exception. In the study of political scientists previously cited, the top 19 perceived influentials were listed; the two who are in our sample, Karl Deutsch and Hans Morgenthau, are also on our list of perceived influentials.[10]

Identification with an academic discipline (unless national security policy is regarded as one, but the respondents did not do so) would seem to make it more difficult to achieve eminence in an area like strategy and disarmament outside of that discipline. After all, identification with a discipline usually involves some consideration of one's disciplinary colleagues as a potential audience, and this may well conflict with either a client such as the government or with the audience of others working in strategy

Table 5

PERCEIVED INFLUENTIALS, DATE OF BIRTH, AND IDENTIFICATION WITH ACADEMIC DISCIPLINE*

Date of Birth	Perceived Influentials		Others		Significance Level
	%	N	%	N	
1900-1919	95	21	46	54	.001
1920-1939	91	11	70	71	NS

* Percentage answering "Yes" to question, "Do you consider yourself affiliated with an academic discipline?"

10. Somit and Tanenhaus, *American Political Science*, p. 66.

and disarmament but with different disciplinary identifications.[11] However, identification with an academic discipline was related to perceived influential status among the older respondents, as shown in Table 5; the difference was much less among the younger group, again because of the change of the younger non-influentials.

The pattern on all three of these variables was the same. Among the older age group, the perceived influentials were more "academically" oriented than the remainder of the group; among the younger respondents, the differences were less, usually not significant. The differences between the two age groups is due to the younger non-influentials' having become more academically oriented than their older counterparts. We cannot infer a causal relationship here, although it is tempting to view this as an example of the role of the perceived influentials as a "leading group" for the rest of the sample. At any rate, this shift did reduce a potentially important division between the perceived influentials and the other members of the sample. As we shall see below, it proved difficult to discern any other such divisions.

influence and the influentials

One of the difficulties of this study is its inability to measure empirically whether the population has had any real effect on American foreign and military policy. Since satisfaction and frustration patterns were also concerns, however, it seemed only logical to ask the respondents what they thought. We have already seen that, when asked what individuals had made the most important contribution to the field, they tended to name members of the population. Two more questions related to this problem; they concerned the influence of the group as a whole and of the particular respondent as an individual.

11. For valuable further discussion of the problem of audiences, see Archibald, *Social Conflict*, chap. 5, pp. 12–31, and chap. 6, pp. 8–9, 12–13, 17–19, 39.

The sample had a high opinion of its influence, both individually and collectively. Table 6 shows that on both indicators the perceived influentials tended to see themselves as having more influence but that the differences between them and the rest of the sample were not statistically significant. This is especially

Table 6

**PERCEIVED INFLUENTIALS AND GROUP
AND PERSONAL SUBJECTIVE INFLUENCE**

Query and Response	Perceived Influentials	Others
"How much would you say civilians not employed by the government have influenced American defense policy since World War II?"*		
"A good deal" or "very much".............	67%	54%
"Somewhat"............................	23%	27%
"Not very much" or "not at all".............	8%	15%
"Don't know"...........................	2%	4%
Total................................	100%	100%
(Number)	(39)	(144)
"Do you think that you as an individual have ever significantly influenced a policy of the United States government in the field of strategy and disarmament?"†		
Yes..................................	50%	39%
No...................................	18%	39%
Don't know............................	32%	22%
Total................................	100%	100%
(Number)	(38)	(145)

* Significance level: NS

† Significance level: .15

interesting on the second indicator, concerning personal influence; the lack of difference may be due to the particular question, since conceivably perceived influentials may have influenced more than one such decision.

Nevertheless, it is striking that, of the respondents who said that they had significantly influenced a government policy, 70 percent were *not* perceived influentials. It appears that the "non-influentials" do not see their chances of influencing government policy foreclosed by the existence of the perceived influentials; this, in turn, would suggest that a potential friction point between these two groups may not exist. This conclusion, however, must remain tentative, since frustration is the product of tension between perceived efficacy and expectations, and so far we have probed only one aspect of this combination.

Unfortunately, no specific questions were included as to the vehicles by which this influence was exercised. One possibility is the government research contract in nuclear strategy and disarmament. It was expected that the perceived influentials would be more likely to have worked on such contracts, and this proved true; 67 percent of their number, as opposed to 41 percent of the rest of the sample, answered this question affirmatively (Ns were 39 and 150 respectively, and the difference was significant at the .05 level).

policy attitudes

Any differences in attitudes on foreign and military policy between the perceived influentials and the remainder of the sample are of interest for at least two reasons. In the first place, if the influentials occupy the position of a "leading group," this may give us a clue as to future changes of opinion of the sample as a whole. Second, the analyses of the policy attitudes of the private nuclear strategists have been based upon the opinions of members of the perceived influentials;[12] if there are differences between

12. Robert A. Levine and Arthur Herzog.

the two groups, we would cast doubts on the basis of these analyses.

As expected, there were no significant differences in policy attitudes between the perceived influentials and the remainder of the sample. Table 7 shows all of the policy attitude questions on our questionnaire, with the differences in the responses of the two groups. With the exception of two questions, all of these questions were answered on a seven-point agree-disagree scale; the responses were collapsed into a three-point scale: agree, neither agree nor disagree, and disagree. All questions were double coded, to include comments or reservations; when these indicated that the answer was not appropriate for any reason (misunderstanding of the question, changing the question, and so on), the response was deleted from this table, as were "don't know" answers. The same procedure was followed throughout the study with these policy questions.

Table 7 indicates that one policy attitude, the short-term relative threat of China and the Soviet Union, revealed a difference between the perceived influentials and the rest of the sample that was statistically significant; however, this relationship was accounted for by the ex-military respondents.[13]

It was concluded that there were no significant differences in policy attitudes between the perceived influentials and the remainder of the sample; this, in turn, reinforced the general conclusion that, with the exception of publication points and age, other differences between the two groups were not important.

The significance of these findings is pointed up by comparison with another viewpoint. Philip Green, in an impressive piece of analysis,[14] argues that in order to influence government policy one must have access and time, resources that are in fact possessed by a very few people. Several points suggest themselves. Pre-

13. The ex-military respondents, including their policy attitudes, will be discussed in detail in the next chapter.

14. Philip Green, "Science, Government, and the Case of RAND: A Singular Pluralism," *World Politics* 20 (1968), 301–26.

Table 7

PERCEIVED INFLUENTIALS AND AGREEMENT
WITH POLICY STATEMENTS

Statement	Perceived Influentials		Others		Significance Level
	%	N	%	N	
American foreign policy since World War II has not faced up to the fundamental problem of a hostile Communist foe dedicated to its destruction.........................	14	35	9	129	NS
American foreign policy since World War II has placed too much emphasis on the threat of world communism and the Soviet bloc..................	67	33	70	135	NS
The aggressive tendencies of the Soviet Union have been greatly reduced since World War II...........	78	32	76	136	NS
In ten years China will be a greater threat to the United States than the Soviet Union will be...............	30	27	57	116	.05
It seems likely that, within this century, the Soviet Union and the United Sates will be allied against China..........	43	7	41	29	NS
The major threat to American national interests abroad since World War II has been Russian and Chinese national power rather than communist ideology.*.........................	71	28	73	117	NS
The present system of deterrence seems unlikely to last until the end of the century without breaking down into a central nuclear war...........	45	29	51	109	NS
The American policy of containment of the Soviet Union has been a success.	82	28	68	138	.20
Percentage that has publicly disagreed with a U.S. government position on strategy and disarmament within the past five years.*..................	94	36	86	136	NS

* Questionnaire asked for dichotomous rather than seven-point response.

Table 7 —*Continued*

Statement	Perceived Influentials		Others		Significance Level
	%	N	%	N	
In the nuclear age, the American government must regard itself as being responsible, not only to the American people, but also to the people of the world.	94	33	91	140	NS
Some form of world government is the only long-term solution to the problem of destructiveness of modern weapons and opposing nationalisms.	50	28	66	137	.20

sumably these few people get their ideas from somewhere, so influence might be indirect; however, we have no way of testing this idea. On a deeper level our sample seems to disagree with Green's implicit assumption that the only way to really influence government policy is by research contract, since 33 percent of the perceived influentials had never worked on such a contract. Lastly, even if Green's theory is correct, the lack of significant policy differences between the influentials and the remainder of the sample suggests that it may not make much difference.

patterns of choice of perceived influentials

So far in our study of the perceived influentials we have been concerned with who was chosen. Before leaving the topic, however, one other facet should be explored briefly: who chose whom? The initial central hypothesis was that the population was composed of several distinct subgroups, each with similar motives for entering the field, employment experience, background factors, policy attitudes, and their own sets of perceived influentials. It was therefore expected that a *few* distinct groups of influentials would emerge from a sociometric analysis; the existence of a RAND group, a peace research group, a Pennsylvania (Foreign Policy Research Institute) group, among others, was predicted. Instead, a *large number of small but distinct groups* was found.

Methodology in sociometry is varied and does not always give comparable results. However, factor analysis of a chooser-chosen matrix has shown some advantages over other possible techniques.[15] Through the courtesy of Professor Duncan MacRae, Jr., and the University of Chicago Computer Center, a copy of the program UCSL 312 was obtained, a factor analysis sociometry program written by Brian Berry.[16] Because it is written for a square matrix, all of the sample could not be included in it; the computer available (IBM 7094/7040) could not handle a 191 x 191 matrix. A somewhat crude technique was devised, therefore, that did permit all of the sample to be included. This consisted simply in taking the same type of binary matrix used as input by the Chicago program and performing a standard factor analysis on it.[17] This allowed for the use of a rectangular matrix.

In order to test the technique, both the Chicago program and the one devised were first used on the same data, a 40 x 40 binary matrix formed by the perceived influentials in the sample and *their* choices of influentials. Table 8 presents the results of these two analyses so that comparison may be facilitated. All individuals loading over .30 on a factor in either program were included. The Yale factor analysis program isolated six factors; the Chicago program produced fourteen. However, the first six of the Chicago program were similar to those of the Yale program. The

15. See Duncan MacRae, Jr., "Direct Factor Analysis of Sociometric Data," *Sociometry* 23 (1960), 360–71, and Terrance Nosanchuk, "A Comparison of Several Sociometric Partitioning Techniques," *Sociometry* 26 (1963), 112–24.

16. The program performs a factor analysis of a binary choice matrix, using the Cholesky decomposition method, a square root technique, and varimax rotation of factors with one or more high loadings. Note that in constructing the binary choice matrices, in opposition to the usual practice, self-choices are included.

17. The factor analysis program used was Yale Computer Center's No. 6S, using the principal axis method and varimax rotation of factors with eigenvalues equal to, or greater than, one.

last eight factors all had one member apiece; in order, they were: Grenville Clark, Karl W. Deutsch, Thomas K. Finletter, Jerome D. Frank, Raymond L. Garthoff, Morton H. Halperin, Bernhard G. Bechhoefer, and Marvin I. Kalkstein.

Table 8
FACTORS AND FACTOR LOADINGS IN CHICAGO AND YALE FACTOR ANALYSIS SOCIOMETRY PROGRAMS OF PERCEIVED INFLUENTIALS

	Chicago	Yale
Factor 1		
Anatol Rapoport	1.00	.88
Emile Benoit	.58	.67
Kenneth Boulding	.58	.83
Walter Millis	.58	.62
Factor 2		
Herman Kahn	1.00	.53
Thomas C. Schelling	.61	.38
Bernard Brodie	.35	
William Kaufmann	.35	
Donald Brennan	.33	
Charles E. Osgodd	.33	
Malcolm W. Hoag		.85
Factor 3		
Hans J. Morgenthau	.97	.90
Charles E. Osgood	.65	.91
Herman Kahn		.36
Factor 4		
J. David Singer	.99	.83
Louis B. Sohn	.37	.77
Kenneth Boulding	.34	
Factor 5		
William W. Kaufmann	.93	.77
Bernard Brodie	.39	.76
Donald Brennan		.66
Herman Kahn		.43
Factor 6		
Anthony J. Wiener	1.00	.56
Thomas C. Schelling		.77
Emile Benoit		.36
Walter Millis		−.42

The factors in Table 8 are listed in the order in which they appeared in the Chicago program. The Yale program gave them in a slightly different order, but the difference was not great. The Yale procedure also gave the percentage of the variance explained by each factor; it ranged from 6 percent to 3 percent, with all six totaling only 25 percent.

Table 8 shows that, of the 25 individuals who loaded over .30 on *either* program, 13, or slightly more than half, loaded on *both*. Moreover, of the 12 that appeared only in one program, only 3 had a score of over .50, and no two of these were on the same factor. It must be remembered that the two programs used different factor analysis techniques.[18] It was concluded that the two techniques had produced essentially the same results, and that the technique devised for the study could be used with more confidence.

Once again, a binary choice matrix was constructed, this time using the choices of the 191 members of the sample. As previously mentioned, 84 individuals were named by one or more respondents other than themselves. Since the factor analysis chosen was limited to 70 variables, only the 44 who were named by two or more respondents were included. (Note that this is not the same group as the 40 perceived influentials in the sample, who have been the subject of this chapter; the group of 44 included some who had not returned the questionnaire.) The same factor analysis program was used on the 44 x 191 matrix. The process isolated no fewer than *twenty* factors. Table 9 shows these factors in the order of their percentage of variance, with individuals who loaded at .30 or higher on each. In a few cases the temptation to name the factors was irresistible; however, no attempt was made to do so for the entire group of twenty. Most of the factors make sense, although they were not all readily predictable. One striking example is Hans Bethe, who is linked with Jerome Wiesner on Factor

---

18. For further discussion and references, see Harry H. Harman, *Modern Factor Analysis* (Chicago: University of Chicago Press, 1960), pp. 102–3, 109–11, 114–16, 154–91.

Table 9
**FACTORS AND FACTOR LOADINGS IN FACTOR ANALYSIS
OF CHOICE OF PERCEIVED INFLUENTIALS**

	Factor Loadings	Percentage Variance
Factor 1 (Pennsylvania-F.P.R.I.)		5%
William R. Kintner	.93	
Stefan T. Possony	.88	
Robert Strausz-Hupe	.58	
Maxwell Taylor	.47	
Thomas W. Wolfe	.40	
Factor 2 (Peace Research)		5%
Kenneth E. Boulding	.77	
J. David Singer	.72	
Anatol Rapoport	.66	
Emile Benoit	.62	
Seymour Melman	.40	
Factor 3		4%
Bernhard G. Bechhoefer	.85	
Malcom W. Hoag	.80	
Seymour Melman	.55	
Factor 4 (Classic RAND)		4%
William W. Kaufmann	.76	
Albert J. Wohlstetter	.72	
Herman Kahn	.54	
Thomas C. Schelling	.32	
Factor 5 (Peace Action)		4%
Jerome D. Frank	.86	
A. J. Muste	.78	
Factor 6 (Government Service)		4%
J. Robert Oppenheimer	.78	
Dean Acheson	.71	
Maxwell Taylor	.60	
Factor 7 (World Law)		4%
Grenville Clark	.73	
Louis B. Sohn	.71	
Eugene Rabinowitch	.59	
Factor 8		4%
Fred C. Ikle	.83	
Thomas W. Wolfe	.80	
Factor 9		4%
Hans J. Morgenthau	.85	
Henry S. Rowen	.76	

Table 9 —*Continued*

	Factor Loadings	Percentage Variance
Factor 10		4%
Arthur I. Waskow	.87	
Ralph E. Lapp	.80	
Factor 11		
Amron H. Katz	.89	
Robert Strausz-Hupe	.65	
Charles E. Osgood	.43	
Factor 12		3%
Henry A. Kissinger	.68	
Robert E. Osgood	.63	
Thomas C. Schelling	.45	
Bernard Brodie	.30	
Factor 13		3%
Donald G. Brennan	.79	
Jeremy J. Stone	.74	
Factor 14		3%
Edward Teller	.77	
Hans Bethe	.51	
Charles E. Osgood	.45	
Linus Pauling	.37	
Factor 15		3%
Richard B. Foster	.82	
Thomas C. Schelling	.46	
Albert J. Wohlstetter	.41	
Stefan T. Possony	.32	
Factor 16		3%
Norman Cousins	.81	
Linus Pauling	.67	
Factor 17		3%
Jerome B. Wiesner	.78	
Hans Bethe	.55	
Louis B. Sohn	.34	
Factor 18		3%
Walter Millis	.86	
Seymour Melman	.39	
Bernhard G. Bechhoefer	.31	
Factor 19		3%
William T. R. Fox	.92	
Bernard Brodie	.41	
Factor 20		2%
Paul Ramsey	.83	

17, apparently because they are so much alike, and with Edward Teller on Factor 14 because they are so different. (Respondents linked them together because of their extended debate centering over the nuclear test ban issue.) Some, such as Factor 11, are puzzling combinations. Most of the people chosen as perceived influentials are members of the population, but within the population there are many different divisions rather than a few dominant ones. This in turn suggests that the picture of a few clashing subgroups often cited in the literature and in discussion may be a myth; indeed, later chapters will show remarkably little evidence of such major cleavages within the sample.

soldiers and civilians

The relationship between the civilian strategists and the professional soldier has two major aspects of interest here. In the first place, the military is one of two major competitors of the private strategists (the other being the public civilian strategists, those employed by the government). But it is also a source of recruitment; given a military system that retires a large number of its officers at an age when a second career is desirable for both personal and economic reasons, continuing to work in the area of strategy after retirement is obviously an attractive alternative for at least some individuals. (The same system, of course, makes it almost impossible to reverse the process; it thus allows the private nuclear strategists to include significant numbers of former members of both competing groups, giving it a potential breadth beyond the others, in keeping with the private strategists' advisory status and lack of command responsibility.) We will examine each of these facets in turn.

soldiers versus civilians

We have seen earlier that before World War II the strategic community, for all intents and purposes, was contiguous to the professional military; whatever influence the civilian strategists (public and private) have had on government policy has necessarily come largely at the expense of the military. This influence has come in two different ways; at the same time civilians (although by no means always the same ones) have practically created the field of arms control and have made disarmament a respectable subject, while also making contributions in military strategy per se. Both present potential although differing threats to the professional military; the first may lessen or at least alter the military function, whereas the latter may more easily be seen as a supplement to, rather than a replacement for, the military.

Indeed, it is important to note that this conflict is a limited one, especially on the part of civilians. There seems to be no sentiment that the military should be replaced by civilians; no one has suggested putting RAND people in command of platoons in Vietnam, for instance. The few members of the strategic community who talk about abolishing the military want to eliminate the military *function* through a system of world disarmament. Similarly, the universities seem likely to remain the sanctuaries of civilians, and few military men show any reluctance to read and use civilian studies of strategy when they support their own positions. The research institutes, after all, were set up by the military and in general retain their financial dependence upon it.[1] The competition is over status and influence on government policy, and it is with this conflict that we are concerned.

Because of this conflict the sample was expected to oppose increasing the influence of the military in government policy, and this appears to be true. There were two questions concerned with this hypothesis. Question 29 stated:

1. Smith, *RAND Corporation*, pp. 125–39; Lyons and Morton, *Schools for Strategy*, pp. 231–64.

Please indicate opposite each field of study whether you believe that *in the past* its general influence in the area of nuclear strategy and disarmament has been too great, too small, or about right.

Responses were requested on a five-point scale to twenty entries. The first three were general areas (physical sciences, social sciences, and humanities); the other seventeen were academic and professional fields. One of these was "military and naval science." The second indicator was a seven-point agree-disagree scale response to Question 51, which read:

The military should have a greater voice in strategic decisions than it has today.

Fifty-one percent of the sample felt that the influence of military and naval science had been too great in the past, and 72 percent said that the military should not have a larger voice in strategic decisions. In contrast, 24 percent said military and naval science had had too little influence, and 19 percent said that the military should have a greater voice (Ns were 134 and 170 respectively). Given the competitive nature of the professional military and our population, this was the expected response.

It was also expected that dislike for the military would increase with higher education, reflecting the cliché that academics in general tend to be strongly opposed to the military. However, as shown in Table 10, this was only partly true. On the first indicator those with master's degrees were actually promilitary, whereas on the second one there was little difference between those with bachelor's and master's degrees. Both indicate that those with doctorates were, as a group, the most opposed to increased military influence, but in both the difference was not statistically significant.

This difference became important when examining another hypothesis: that the perceived influentials would be more sympathetic toward the military than the rest of the population. It seemed likely that extreme antimilitary feelings would be

Table 10

LEVEL OF EDUCATION AND ATTITUDE TOWARD MILITARY

Opinion on influence of military and naval science in the past on nuclear strategy and disarmament*

Academic Degree	N	Too Great	About Right	Too Small	Total
Bachelor's	36	50%	25%	25%	100%
Master's	24	33	29	38	100
Doctorate	58	62	22	16	100
Professional	9	45	33	22	100

Military should have a larger voice in strategic decisions †

Academic Degree	N	Agree	Neither Agree Nor Disagree	Disagree	Total
Bachelor's	44	25%	9%	66%	100%
Master's	28	25	11	64	100
Doctorate	79	8	6	86	100
Professional	8	13	12	75	100

* Significance level: .20

† Significance level: .15

stronger among individuals who felt themselves cut off from influence and were helpless to do anything about it. Without giving the figures, it appeared at first that this was not true; dividing the sample into influentials and others, there was a difference in the anticipated direction only on one of the two indicators, and even in this case it was quite small. However, this was partially due to the prevalence of doctoral degrees among the influentials, as noted in the previous chapters; when level of education is controlled, the hypothesis is supported. Since there were only three holders of bachelor's degrees and four with master's who were influentials and who answered one of the military attitude questions, no conclusions can be drawn concerning these groups. However, Table 11 shows that, among those who hold doctoral degrees, the influentials were less anti-military than the remainder of the sample, although this difference is significant only on the second indicator. It should be noted that the difference is only one of degree; the perceived influentials were not promilitary, but just somewhat less anti-military. Given the competitive nature of the two groups, this is perhaps not surprising.

Table 11

**RESPONDENTS WITH DOCTORAL DEGREES
AND ATTITUDE TOWARD MILITARY**

Opinion on influence of military and naval science in the past on nuclear strategy and disarmament*

Group	N	Too Great	About Right	Too Small	Total
Perceived Influentials	15	47%	40%	13%	100%
Others	42	69	17	14	100

Military should have a larger voice in strategic decisions†

Group	N	Agree	Neither Agree Nor Disagree	Disagree	Total
Perceived Influentials	23	17%	13%	70%	100%
Others	55	4	4	92	100

* Significance level: .20

† Significance level: .05

soldiers who became civilians

The data confirm the hypothesis that a major source of recruits for the sample has been its major competitor, the professional military. We have already noted the system of early retirement that makes such talent available.[2] It is also worth noting that if the military officer disagrees with government decisions, the traditional restraints of the military profession severely limit his freedom to publicize his opposition and especially to enter partisan politics to support different policies.[3] His traditional recourse has been to resign and then to agitate from the outside.

Criteria for membership in the study population did not exclude men who had been members of the armed forces if they had written in the field when they were not in the service. The fact that most of our sample had been eligible for military service during World War II was reflected in the 102 individuals (55 percent of the sample) who had served in the armed forces. Clearly not all of these could be considered members of the professional military, but it was somewhat difficult to determine a cutting point. Relying on Samuel P. Huntington's distinction between officers, who practice the military *profession*, and enlisted men, who practice the military *trade*,[4] it was decided to limit our group to those who had been officers. Given the tendency of significant numbers of individuals to serve as reserve officers for a few years, usually at low ranks,[5] we further limited the group called "ex-military" in the remainder of this study to those who had attained the rank of captain (army or air force) or lieutenant commander (navy) or above. Forty-two individuals (22 percent of the sample) qualified using this criterion.

One result of the introduction of a significant number of civilians into the strategic community has been a breakdown of

2. For a thorough study of the similar problem of the British armed services see Philip Abrams, "Democracy, Technology, and the Retired British Officer," in Samuel P. Huntington, ed., *Changing Patterns of Military Politics*, International Yearbook of Political Behaviour Research, Vol. 3 (New York: Free Press of Glencoe, Inc., 1962), pp. 150–89; see also Janowitz, *The Professional Soldier*, pp. 372–82.

3. Janowitz, *The Professional Soldier*, pp. 233–36; Samuel P. Huntington, *Soldier and the State*, pp. 14–16.

4. *Soldier and the State*, pp. 17–18.

5. Ibid., p. 17; Janowitz, *The Professional Soldier*, pp. 54–60.

soldier-civilian differences; soldiers have become more civilian-ized, and civilians have become more military.[6] The logical result of this tendency would be to make the distinction between the ex-military members of the sample and the remainder of the group negligible. It was felt, however, that this process had not yet gone so far (assuming that it is proceeding in that direction) and that the division would remain significant; this hypothesis was supported by the data.

It seemed likely that the ex-military members of the population would be, because of their previous affiliation with a competing skill group, an underprivileged and unhappy subgroup. No evidence of such feelings was found, however; in general, ex-military men seemed to be doing quite well within their second vocation. Specifically, they concentrated more in strategy and disarmament, and by nearly all measurements, they occupied a leading, although not dominant, position as compared with the rest of the sample.

Table 12 shows one measurement of this concentration. It was also shown by their identification with specialty areas within an academic discipline. As might be expected, the percentage of ex-military men who regarded themselves as affiliated with an academic discipline was less than the rest of the sample: 54 percent as compared with 69 percent (Ns were 39 and 138). How-

Table 12

**EX-MILITARY AND PERCENTAGE OF PROFESSIONAL TIME
CURRENTLY SPENT IN STRATEGY AND DISARMAMENT**

Group	N	Time Spent				
		0-25%	26-50%	51-75%	76-100%	Total
Ex-military	41	39%	20%	12%	29%	100%
Others	143	62	12	11	15	100

Significance level: .05

6. Lyons, "The New Civil-Military Relations," pp. 53–63; Smith, *RAND Corporation*, pp. 20–29; Janowitz, *The Professional Soldier*, pp. 7–16.

ever, of those who did regard themselves as being part of a discipline, 56 percent of the ex-military men said that they had specialized in an area specifically concerned with strategy and/or disarmament, as compared with only 21 percent of the rest of the sample (Ns were 18 and 87, and the difference was significant at the .01 level).

This concentration may account in part for their prominent position within the sample. As previously noted, 22 percent of the sample was classified as ex-military; however, 31 percent of the perceived influentials were so classified. They had higher publication point scores than the rest of the population, but the difference was not significant. However, the publication point scores exclude any material written while the individual was in the service. They seemed somewhat more confident of their individual efficacy and influence on government policy than the remainder of the sample, although once again the difference was not significant; 68 percent said that they had significantly influenced a government policy in the field of strategy and disarmament, as opposed to 50 percent of the rest of the sample (Ns were 31 and 104, and the significance level was .10).

They consistently represented a slightly disproportionate portion of those who had worked for over four months in the area of strategy and disarmament at all the various types of institutions mentioned (except for college teaching, which will be discussed separately) as shown in Table 13, although none of the differences were statistically significant.

The one exception to this pattern was in the area of college teaching, and the change there was only a relative one. Rather than falling behind the rest of the sample, the ex-military group just about held its own, despite the major handicap of a relative lack of nonmedical doctoral degrees. Of the ex-military group 31 percent held such degrees, as compared with 51 percent of the rest of the sample, and in the American university system this might be expected to be crucial. However, ex-military men made up 21 percent of those who had worked for four months or more in strategy and disarmament at a college or university with teach-

ing responsibilities, as shown in Table 13. They made up 23 percent of all those who had taught a college course in strategy and
disarmament (N was 30), which compares well with their 22 percent of the sample. Moreover, their desires in this area seemed
to have been fulfilled; only 20 percent of the ex-military group
had not taught such a course but would like to in the future, as
compared with 44 percent of the rest of the sample (Ns were
30 and 93).

Table 13

EX-MILITARY AND EMPLOYMENT BY INSTITUTIONS*

	Number	Ex-Military	Others	Significance Level
College or university (teaching full or part time).............................	44	21%	79%	NS
College or university (no teaching)............	19	32	68	NS
Private, nonprofit research institute............	63	27	73	NS
Research institute affiliated with a college or university......................	28	36	64	.15
Private corporation (not nonprofit)............	16	31	69	NS
Periodical (privately owned).................	18	33	67	NS
Federal government........................	35	34	66	.15

* For the sample as a whole (N-191) 22 percent of the ex-military were employed by such
institutions, as compared with 78 percent of the rest of the sample.

The ex-military group did *not* have a dominant position within
the sample. None of the indexes examined showed them occupy-
ing as much as one-half of the most powerful or influential positions within the sample. Moreover, in some important areas they
did not have an advantage over the rest of the sample; 46 percent of them, for instance, had worked on a government research
contract in the area of strategy and disarmament, as compared

with 47 percent of the rest of the population (Ns were 41 and 145). The pattern is one of prominence rather than dominance (even less in the field of college teaching), and this may be due simply to their previous experience in the field.

It was hypothesized that the ex-military members of the sample would be more promilitary and more concerned about the challenge to the United States of world communism in general and the Soviet Union in particular.[7] Both of these positions were supported by the data. The reasoning behind the hypothesis as to the promilitary tendencies of the ex-military group is obvious enough, and the results can be quickly summarized in Table 14.

Table 14

EX-MILITARY AND ATTITUDE TOWARD MILITARY

Opinion on influence of military and naval science in the past on nuclear strategy and disarmament*

Group	N	Too Great	About Right	Too Small	Total
Ex-military	30	37%	16%	47%	100%
Others	101	55	27	18	100

Military should have larger voice in strategic decisions†

Group	N	Agree	Neither Agree nor Disagree	Disagree	Total
Ex-military	37	51%	8%	41%	100%
Others	128	8	8	84	100

* Significance level: .01

† Significance level: .001

An equally interesting confirmation of this hypothesis may be found by studying the percentages in the table by column rather than by row. The ex-military men made up 23 percent and 22 percent respectively of all those answering these two questions,

7. Janowitz, *The Professional Soldier*, pp. 233–79, 303–44.

but they accounted for 44 percent and 65 percent of the pro-military responses on them.

Despite these differences on the desirability of increasing military influence, the two groups had almost identical views on the past influence of civilians outside of government. Sixty-one percent of the ex-military thought they had had either a good deal or very much influence; 13 percent thought they had had either none at all or not very much; comparable figures for the rest of the sample were 59 percent and 14 percent (Ns were 39 and 135). If civilians outside of government and the professional military were the only two groups in the strategic community, we could conclude that the two subgroups held similar views on the *actual* balance of influence but that they differ in their views of a *desirable* balance. Unfortunately this is too strong a conclusion for the data; the existence of civilians inside the government as the third major group in the strategic community makes it possible that both subgroups may have identical views on the desirable role of private civilian strategists and differ only on that of the public ones.

Table 15 shows the data resulting from four attitude questions relating to world communism and the Soviet Union (questions 52, 48, 54, and 62). Given the rather crude nature of the instruments, it would be unwise to put too much emphasis on any one indicator; however, the fact that all four vary in the same direction gives strong support to the hypothesis.

It is in the light of this background that two questions relating to the relative magnitude of the threats to the United States of the Soviet Union and Communist China must be examined. It was expected that, since the military was so concerned about communism in general and the Soviet Union, it would regard China as less of a threat than the senior member of the Soviet bloc. If one is concerned primarily about communist ideology and feels that the intentions of the Soviet Union and China are the same, it is clear that Russia is a much more dangerous adversary, since it has greater national power at its disposal. These expectations were confirmed. Two questions concerned this

Table 15

EX-MILITARY AND ATTITUDES TOWARD
COMMUNISM AND THE SOVIET UNION

Group	N	Agree	Neither Agree Nor Disagree	Disagree	Total
American foreign policy since World War II has not faced up to the fundamental problem of a hostile communist foe dedicated to its destruction.*					
Ex-military	34	26%	3%	71%	100%
Others	128	5	8	87	100
American foreign policy since World War II has placed too much emphasis on the threat of world communism and the Soviet bloc.*					
Ex-military	37	41%	5%	54%	100%
Others	129	78	5	17	100
The aggressive tendencies of the Soviet Union have been greatly reduced since World War II.*					
Ex-military	34	47%	6%	47%	100%
Others	133	84	6	10	100

The major threat to American national interests abroad since World War II has been†

Group	N	Communist Ideology‡	Both or Other	Russian and Chinese National Power	Total
Ex-military	36	33%	22%	47%	100%
Other	125	12	21	67	100

* Significance level: .001

† Significance level: .01

‡ On the questionnaire, respondents were requested to choose one of the two alternatives. However, enough qualified their answers that they were coded on a five-point scale. This table includes both those who chose on alternative and those who indicated that one was more important than the other, although they could not be separated.

hypothesis; both were statements with seven-point agree-disagree scale responses. Question 50 stated:

In ten years China will be a greater threat to the United States than the Soviet Union will be.

Thirty-three percent of the ex-military agreed, and 67 percent disagreed; comparable figures for the remainder of the sample were 56 percent and 31 percent (Ns were 30 and 111; significance level was .01). Question 53 stated:

It seems likely that, within this century, the Soviet Union and the United States will be allied against China.

The ex-military group divided evenly on this question; 40 percent agreed, and 40 percent disagreed. However, the rest of the population was not so undecided; 55 percent agreed, and 32 percent disagreed (Ns were 30 and 109, but the difference was not significant).

This concern with the Soviet Union and world communism may be related to the fact that the ex-military group seemed less concerned that the present system of deterrence might result in a central nuclear war. Robert Levine has based his taxonomy of the arms debate on the tension between the fear of communism and the fear of thermonuclear war,[8] and it is interesting to note that there does seem to be some relationship between these two in our study. Question 51 asserted:

The present system of deterrence seems unlikely to last until the end of the century without breaking down in a central nuclear war.

Forty percent of the ex-military agreed with this statement, but 57 percent disagreed; comparable figures for the rest of the population were 51 percent and 40 percent (Ns were 30 and 107).

However, it would be unwise to overestimate the magnitude or significance of the differences between the ex-military and the remainder of the population. There are significant groups within the ex-military that hold views much like those of the

8. Levine, *The Arms Debate*, pp. 44–57.

remainder of the sample. Moreover, even though individuals may take different positions on the magnitude of the threats to be combatted, they may agree on the measures to be taken. This is perhaps especially likely to be true in a political system based on compromise such as ours; it is a tribute to the ability of American foreign policy to be all things to all men that there seems to be general approval of its past tendencies. Question 55 stated:

The American policy of containment of the Soviet Union has been a success.

Seventy-one percent of the ex-military agreed with that statement, and 23 percent disagreed; comparable figures for the rest of the sample were 70 percent and 21 percent (Ns were 34 and 130). With that kind of agreement on general policy, the significance of attitude differences is considerably reduced.

chapter four

motivation and frustration

We have noted previously that the private nuclear strategists are a disparate group in terms of background. The only known common demoninator is their involvement in nuclear strategy and disarmament. Therefore, the motives of the respondents are of interest. By indicating why individuals entered the field, they may suggest under what conditions they are likely to leave it. They may point up the particular problem areas that are likely to be of interest to the population. Used in these ways, they may also give useful insights into the substances of distinctions within the population and some feeling of the dynamics of the relationships of subgroups to the population as a whole.

Granted the desirability of information on motives, however, it was difficult to design an effective instrument to obtain it. Since the field of study is a relatively new one, it seemed unlikely that tradition would play the role it has in certain related areas, especially the military.[1] Moreover, the high educational level of

1. Janowitz, *The Professional Soldier*, pp. 108–24.

the population suggests that it is potentially mobile and that few would have been forced to work in this field. This in turn implies that the decision to work here is one that each individual has made for himself. In one sense it is impossible to make any meaningful statements on the subject without the use of depth psychology; the motives for entering the field are undoubtedly as numerous as the population. However, it is not necessary to probe so deeply into the individual for our purposes. Acknowledging the complexity of the topic, it seemed desirable to keep the instrument as simple as possible. Question 32 stated:

Opposite each of the following possible reasons for doing work in the area of strategy and disarmament, please indicate whether it had not much influence, some influence, or very much influence on *your* decision to *enter* the field.

Twenty reasons were listed, the last being "other." Each was followed by space to check one of the three alternative responses. These reasons, with the percentage answering "very much or some" or "very much" are given in Table 16, in order of their frequency.[2]

They may be divided into motives (internal factors) and influences (external factors).[3] We may further divide motives into policy and academic ones. This gives three groups of reasons: policy motives (threat of modern weapons, altering American foreign policy, desire for world disarmament, concern about moral problems of American policy, threat of world communism, and desire to promote democracy); academic motives (intellectual interest, spreading knowledge, and influencing young minds); and influences (World War II, a specific job opportu-

---

2. For those interested in the order in which these alternatives appeared on the questionnaire, see Appendix B. Some attempt was made when the questionnaire was constructed to arrange the items in descending order of expected importance, in order to reduce anticipated hostility to the question.

3. This distinction is one of several that I owe to observations by respondents to the questionnaire.

Table 16

REASONS FOR WORKING IN STRATEGY AND DISARMAMENT

Reason	N	Very Much	Very Much or Some
Concern about threat of modern weapons to the human race............	159	65%	87%
Intellectual interest in international affairs.......................	150	64	88
Desire to significantly alter American foreign policy....................	159	40	75
Desire to encourage world disarmament..............................	155	34	66
Desire to teach and disseminate knowledge in area....................	150	34	71
Concern about moral problems of current American military policy.........	148	32	63
Desire to influence young minds...........	143	20	52
Experiences during World War II...........	142	20	41
Specific job opportunity.................	133	20	49
Related problem in another field...........	128	19	46
Desire to combat world communism........	145	16	37
Influence of individual working in field.....................................	132	14	45
Desire to promote democracy throughout world.....................	137	12	44
Influence of book or publication in field...............................	130	9	28
Casual exposure to area.................	122	7	38
Availability of research funds in field.....................................	128	2	23
Influence of individual not working in field...........................	118	3	9
College course in field...................	124	2	11
College course in another field that included section on area............	128	2	13
Other..	28	89	100

nity, related problem in another field, a publication in the field, availability of research funds, a person or college course in or out of the field, and casual exposure to the area). Table 16 suggests that motives have been much more important than influences and that the conflict between academic and policy aspects of the subject continues in the area of motivation; perhaps it would be more accurate to say that it begins as early as motives for doing work in the field. Using averages to compensate for the smaller number of academic motives listed, academic motives were listed as having had "very much" influence by an average of 58 individuals, as compared with 51 for policy motives and 13 for influences. This implies that entrance to the field for most respondents was a deliberate decision rather than a fortuitous combination of circumstances.

Although this expected duality was reflected in the data, another was not. It was noted in the preceding chapter that Robert Levine, in his discussion of policy positions in strategy and disarmament, regarded concern for nuclear war and communism as the two major elements of his theoretical framework. Concern about the threat of nuclear weapons was one of the two most important motives, with 65 percent regarding it as having had "very much" influence and 88 percent as having either "very much" or "some" influence on their decisions to enter the field. However, concern about world communism ranked only eleventh among twenty reasons, and eighth among nine motives; only 16 percent said it had "very much" influence, and only 37 percent said it had "very much" or "some." It would be inappropriate to conclude that the large majority of the population could consequently be included in Levine's "antiwar" groups; there is a difference between the intellectual bases of theory and the motives for doing work in a field, and we have no way of telling whether significant changes take place after an individual enters the area. Nevertheless, the sample would appear to be exceedingly unpromising material for an anticommunist nuclear crusade.

patterns of motives and influences

Although Table 16 gives some interesting information about reasons for working in strategy and disarmament, it says nothing about the relationships among these reasons. In line with the basic hypothesis, a few (four or five at most) rather distinct patterns of motives were predicted that would account for most of the variance; thus most individuals could be classified into one of these groups. In order to test this hypothesis, a factor analysis was performed on the twenty variables listed in Table 16,[4] the results of which are shown in Table 17. It yielded seven factors; the table includes all factor loadings larger than .40. The factors themselves were fairly well delineated, with reasonably high loadings on enough variables so that they could be interpreted with some confidence; on the basis of the variables involved, they were named as shown in the table.

However, they did not account for much of the variance; the largest factor accounted for only 14 percent, and all seven picked up only 65 percent. The significance of these figures, like many in this study, is subject to personal interpretation. The hypothesis was rejected, even though several distinct groups of motives and influences could be separated out, because all of the factors together accounted for only two-thirds of the variance. This by no means guarantees unity in any sense of the word; after all, individuals with similar motives can disagree violently. But one major hypothetical internal barrier of our population was less important than expected.

frustration and fulfillment

Although the data on motivations were of considerable interest, they seemed incomplete in and of themselves. Motivations sug-

4. The program used was Yale Computer Center's No. 6S, using the principal axis method and varimax rotation of factors with eigenvalues equal to, or greater than, one.

Table 17

FACTORS AND FACTOR LOADINGS IN
FACTOR ANALYSIS OF MOTIVES AND INFLUENCES

Motive or Influence	Factor Loadings
Factor 1 (Antiwar policy); 14% of variance	
Desire to encourage world disarmament	.86
Concern about threat of modern weapons to human race	.81
Desire to significantly alter American foreign policy	.80
Concern about moral problems of current American military policy	.57
Factor 2 (Academic, research); 10% of variance	
Specific job opportunity	.71
Availability of research funds in field	.63
Intellectual interest in international security affairs	.58
Casual exposure to area	.50
Related problem in another field	.46
Influence of individual working in field	.44
Factor 3 (Academic, teaching); 10% of variance	
Desire to teach and disseminate knowledge in area	.81
Desire to influence young minds	.75
Concern about moral problems of current American military policy	.52
Intellectual interest in international security affairs	.43
Factor 4 (Impersonal influences); 9% of variance	
College course in another field that included section on area	.86
Influence of book or publication in field	.75
Relation problem in another field	.40
Factor 5 (Ideological); 8% of variance	
Desire to combat world communism	.78
Desire to promote democracy throughout world	.64
Casual exposure to area	-.43
Factor 6 (Personal influences); 8% of variance	
Influence of individual not working in field	.73
College course in field	.67
Influence of individual working in field	.61
Factor 7 (Other); 6% of variance	
Other	.91

gest the expectations with which individuals enter the field, but they do not tell whether these expectations are fulfilled by experience. After all, it is not uncommon for an individual entering a field of work to have to seriously modify his initial expectations. Again, the problem arose of devising an instrument to measure an intricate and personal aspect of the respondents, and again, it was decided to make it as simple as possible. Question 32 read:

Please indicate also whether your *expectations* when you *entered* the field have generally been fulfilled.

This question was placed between Question 31 (which asked about possible reasons for entering the field) and the twenty reasons. Opposite each reason, therefore, were blanks to indicate how much of a factor it had been in deciding to enter the area and also three columns marked "fulfilled," "not fulfilled," and "don't know," to answer Question 32. This arrangement appears to have been somewhat confusing; it also asked respondents to make some drastic oversimplifications to reduce their experience in one of these complex areas to a simple yes or no. This probably accounts for the lower Ns on the second question as opposed to the first.

The results of Question 32 are given in Table 18. (Only motives are listed; influences had even smaller Ns, and in most cases the question of fulfillment was not really relevant.) This table includes two percentage figures. The first is self-explanatory: the percentage of respondents who said their expectations were not fulfilled. The second, called the frustration index, combines information from Tables 16 and 18 into a single statistic. If we regard frustration as the combination of expectations and nonfulfillment, we may construct an index that is the percentage of those answering both questions who felt the motive in question had "very much" influence and that their expectations were "not fulfilled." Thus the fact that 76 percent of those answering the questions about a desire to promote world democracy felt their expectations had not been fulfilled is interesting, but it is less significant than it might seem since Table 16 shows that only 12 percent said it had "very much" influence on their deci-

Table 18

MOTIVES AND FRUSTRATION

	N	Not Fulfilled	Frustration Index
Concern about threat of modern weapons to human race..........	90	59%	52%
Desire to encourage world disarmament...................	69	80	51
Desire to significantly alter American foreign policy..........	82	63	38
Concern about moral problems of current American military policy.......................	56	50	25
Desire to combat world communism.	40	55	23
Desire to promote democracy throughout world................	38	76	16
Desire to influence young minds....	50	20	12
Desire to teach and disseminate knowledge in area..............	74	16	7
Intellectual interest in international security affairs.........	96	7	4

sion to enter the field. The frustration index of 16 percent reflects this fact. It also covers another important point; if 40 percent of the sample is interested in a particular motive and 40 percent has had its expectations fulfilled, it makes a good deal of difference whether the two figures involve the same individuals or not.

It was expected that satisfaction would be higher for academic than for policy motives, and the results shown in Table 18 confirmed this. The difference was especially marked in the fulfilled–not fulfilled distinction; the figures for "not fulfilled" varied from 50 percent to 80 percent for the policy motives, 7 percent to 20 percent for the academic ones. The difference was considerably less in the frustration index figure, which allowed for the lesser interest in certain of the policy motives.

physical scientists and the ex-military

It was hypothesized that two major occupational groups, the physical scientists and the ex-military, would provide contrasting pictures of concern about war and communism. The interest of physical scientists in strategy and disarmament, after all, came as a result of their concern over the use to which the atomic bomb, a product of their expertise, was to be put by their government.[5] Although it is true that there was a major division within the ranks of the physical scientists on this question,[6] symbolized by Edward Teller and J. Robert Oppenheimer, the dominant public image of the physical scientists' approach to strategy has been shaped by events such as the Pugwash Conferences and publications like the *Bulletin of the Atomic Scientists*. It was therefore expected that physical scientists would be more concerned about the threat of nuclear weapons than the rest of the sample. It should be noted that although they were also expected to be less concerned about the threat of communism, this was in fact a separate hypothesis with no necessary connection to the first one.

The number of respondents who said that they considered themselves physical scientists was rather small, which made statistical significance elusive. Interestingly, Table 19 shows only one significant relationship, and this was not included in our hypotheses: physical scientists were less motivated by intellectual interest. The variables mentioned did go in the expected direction. Thus the physical scientists were more influenced by the

5. For further discussion see Gilpin, *American Scientists and Nuclear Weapons Policy*; Smith, *A Peril and a Hope*; Warner R. Schilling, "The H-Bomb Decisions: How to Decide without Actually Choosing," *Political Science Quarterly* 76 (1961), 33–36, 43.

6. Gilpin, *American Scientists and Nuclear Weapons Policy*, pp. 64–111.

Table 19

MOTIVES AND FRUSTRATION
AND PHYSICAL SCIENTISTS

Motive*	Physical Scientist†	N	%	Signif- icance Level	Frustration Index	
					N	%
Concern about threat of modern weapons to hu- man race	Yes No	21 132	81 63	.15	17 70	71 50
Intellectual interest in international security affairs	Yes No	16 129	37 67	.05	11 82	0 5
Desire to significant- ly alter American foreign policy	Yes No	20 131	60 37	.15	14 64	57 33
Desire to encourage world disarmament	Yes No	21 129	52 31	.08	13 53	62 38
Desire to teach and disseminate knowledge in area	Yes No	20 125	15 38	.08	4 68	25 6
Concern about moral problems of current American military pol- icy	Yes No	20 123	35 32	NS	9 44	44 21
Desire to influence young minds	Yes No	18 120	17 20	NS	5 44	20 9
Desire to combat world communism	Yes No	16 124	6 16	.15	4 34	0 24
Desire to promote de- mocracy throughout world	Yes No	16 116	6 13	.15	4 32	0 19

* Figures given are for those who were influenced "very much" by motive.

† Refers to question "Do you regard yourself as physical scientist?"

threat of modern weapons and a desire to encourage world disarmament, and were less concerned about world communism; but differences were notable rather than significant. The reason they were not significant seems to be that the physical scientists were motivated by generally the same motives that influenced the rest of the sample; the only difference was in strength. Statistical significance is more likely to appear when the directions are different. Thus the physical scientists differed from the rest of the sample on both of the two major motives of the sample as a whole. However, the difference was significant only on intellectual interest, where the direction of the physical scientists was opposed to that of the rest of the sample. All in all, the differences were less than had been expected.

In Chapter 3 we discussed at some length the differences between those individuals who had reached the rank of captain (army or air force) or lieutenant commander (navy) or above, whom we have called ex-military, and the remainder of the sample. Among other things, we concluded that as a group they were somewhat more concerned about the threat of communism than the remainder of the sample and somewhat less concerned about the likelihood of central nuclear war, as had been expected. It was expected that these tendencies would be reflected in their motives in entering the field.

Table 20 supports the first hypothesis but not the second. It is true that the ex-military asserted that they were more influenced by a desire to combat world communism than the rest of the sample, as well as being less concerned about encouraging world disarmament. However, on the less controversial question of concern about the threat of modern weapons, the difference was not significant. The difference, then, is not in the recognition of the problem but in the magnitude of the steps that should be taken to deal with it. Indeed, even the ex-military showed more concern for the threat of modern weapons (61 percent) than a desire to combat world communism (39 percent).

Thus we find a similar pattern in both occupational groups that suggests that though the predicted divisions were present, they were not so large that they dominated all other considerations. Although the physical scientists were concerned about the threat of modern weapons more than the rest of the sample as a motive

Table 20

MOTIVES AND FRUSTRATION
AND EX-MILITARY

Motive*	Ex-military†	N	%	Signif-icance Level	Frustration Index	
					N	%
Concern about threat of modern weapons to human race	Yes	31	61	.15	16	63
	No	126	66		72	50
Intellectual interest in international security affairs	Yes	31	77	.15	22	5
	No	117	61		73	4
Desire to significantly alter American foreign policy	Yes	31	39	NS	16	31
	No	126	40		64	39
Desire to encourage world disarmament	Yes	29	17	.05	12	17
	No	124	37		55	46
Desire to teach and disseminate knowledge in area	Yes	30	30	NS	15	7
	No	118	35		57	7
Concern about moral problems of current American military policy	Yes	29	38	NS	11	18
	No	117	31		43	28
Desire to influence young minds	Yes	27	22	NS	12	8
	No	114	19		38	13
Desire to combat world communism	Yes	28	39	.001	12	42
	No	115	10		27	15
Desire to promote democracy throughout world	Yes	26	8	NS	9	0
	No	109	13		28	21

* Figures given are for those who were influenced "very much" by motive.

† Term includes only those who attained the rank of captain (army or air force) or lieutenant commander (navy).

for entering the field, they did not differ much in regard to the impetus of the communist threat. Similarly the ex-military was more concerned about the threat of communism, but it also was impelled by the possible consequences of modern weapons. The pattern of division remains one of differences of emphasis rather than one of kind.

age and government research

The patterns of relationships between the ages of the respondents, their experience in government research contracts, their perceived influence on government policy, their motives in entering the field, and whether or not the latter were fulfilled are rather involved, as shown by Table 21. It had not been expected that age would be a significant variable, but as we shall see, in certain circumstances it became important.

Unlike the previous tables, this one actually involves four variables: motive, fulfillment, age, and whether or not the respondent had worked on a government research contract. The reason for this rather intricate process is that the two independent variables, age and working on a government research contract, were related to one another; younger individuals were more likely to have done such work. For the purpose of this section, age was divided into two groups: those born during the years 1900–1919 and 1920–1939. This included 165 individuals, 86 percent of the respondents; even with groups this large (77 and 88) the Ns in some of the cells were quite small. Of the older group 34 percent had participated in a government research contract in nuclear strategy and disarmament, whereas 63 percent of the younger had. The difference was further reflected in the fact that 68 percent of those who had worked on such a contract were in the younger age group, as compared with 39 percent of those who had not.

Table 21 suggests several interesting patterns of relationships. It appears that individuals who do government research did not feel that American foreign and military policy should be drastically changed. The first three motives—to significantly alter American foreign policy, to encourage world disarmament, and

Table 21

AGE, GOVERNMENT RESEARCH WORK, AND
MOTIVES AND FRUSTRATION

Motive*	Govt.†	Age‡	N	%	Signif-icance Level	Frustration Index	
						N	%
Desire to significant-ly alter American foreign policy	Yes	Older	22	27		10	10
	Yes	Younger	53	23		26	12
	No	Older	46	65		24	67
	No	Younger	26	42	.001	16	58
Desire to encourage world disarmament	Yes	Older	22	18		8	25
	Yes	Younger	53	17		23	17
	No	Older	43	58		16	81
	No	Younger	24	42	.001	15	47
Concern about moral problems of current American military policy	Yes	Older	21	24		7	14
	Yes	Younger	52	17		17	6
	No	Older	39	54		18	44
	No	Younger	24	33	.001	11	27
Desire to combat world communism	Yes	Older	21	24		9	33
	Yes	Younger	54	13		17	18
	No	Older	35	14		7	43
	No	Younger	23	13	.001	5	0
Intellectual interest in international security affairs	Yes	Older	22	68		14	7
	Yes	Younger	54	78		43	29
	No	Older	36	44		14	14
	No	Younger	26	65	.05	16	0
Concern about threat of modern weapons to human race	Yes	Older	23	70		10	100
	Yes	Younger	54	50		34	21
	No	Older	46	74		19	68
	No	Younger	25	80	.10	18	67
Desire to teach and disseminate knowledge in area	Yes	Older	22	41		12	17
	Yes	Younger	54	24		31	3
	No	Older	36	33		13	0
	No	Younger	25	44	NS	13	15
Desire to influence young minds	Yes	Older	22	23		8	13
	Yes	Younger	52	10		19	5
	No	Older	35	20		12	25
	No	Younger	21	29	NS	6	17
Desire to promote de-mocracy throughout world	Yes	Older	22	4		7	14
	Yes	Younger	53	11		16	19
	No	Older	30	17		5	20
	No	Younger	22	9	NS	8	15

* Figures given are for those who were "very much" influenced by motive.

† Refers to question "Have you ever worked on a government research contract in the area of nuclear strategy and disarmament?"

‡ See explanation in text.

concern about moral problems of current American policy—were the strongest policy motives listed. It is clear that the major differences in all three were between those who had done government research and those who had not, although younger members of the latter group tended to be somewhat less concerned about those strong policy motives than their elders. It would be interesting to know whether these people did not work for the government because they did not want to (a few indicated on another question that they would not work for the government as a matter of principle) or because they would not have been allowed to because of their policy attitudes, but there are no data on this point.

The second pattern is shown in the next two variables. Both show decreasing differences over time. Thus the group most concerned about the threat of communism was the older portion of those who had done government research; the difference disappears among the younger respondents. Similarly the group least motivated by intellectual interest was the older portion of those who had not done government research; once again the difference decreases greatly among the younger members of the sample. This probably indicates that as the field of nuclear strategy and disarmament becomes better defined, it tends to exert a more uniform attraction upon its prospective members. However, it is important to remember that this is sharply qualified by the large differences on the three strong policy motives.

employment in nuclear strategy and disarmament

The two major changes in the membership of the strategic community in the United States since World War II have been the introduction of civilians and the rise of institutions other than the federal government as employers of individuals working in the area. The history of the latter process may be found in other studies;[1] without recapitulating it here, it has yielded several different types of institutions with only loose connections rather than a monolithic competitor of the government, a pattern of "strategic pluralism."[2]

It is customary to speak casually of two major institutions, universities and research institutes, as involving most of the civilian strategists. Aside from its simplicity, this duality may also

1. See especially Lyons and Morton, *Schools for Strategy*; Bruce Smith, *The RAND Corporation*.

2. Posvar, "Strategy Expertise and National Security," p. 3, and "The Impact of Strategy Expertise on the National Security Policy of the United States," *Public Policy* 17 (1964), 36–68.

reflect the academic-policy tension discussed earlier. In fact, however, this division does not do justice to the proliferation of institutions employing individuals working in the area. Many universities, for instance, have established research institutes of their own, some of which have done work in strategy and disarmament;[3] the relationship between their personnel and the regular departments varies, but joint appointments tend to be rare and limited to senior members.[4] It is not intuitively obvious whether these institutions are closer to the universities or private research institutes. Similarly, individuals in faculty positions without teaching responsibilities are difficult to classify easily.

Aside from this fissioning within the universities, there are other developments outside of their boundaries. The research institutes that have become well known—among them RAND, the Institute for Defense Analyses, Research Analysis Corporation, Stanford Research Institute, and Hudson Institute—have been nonprofit corporations. However, there are also corporations that are not nonprofit, such as Arthur D. Little, Inc., United Research Inc., and Abt Associates, which do research in the field. Similarly, several major corporations in the aerospace and electronics fields have either established branches specializing in research with a certain amount of autonomy or have done related work within their existing administrative structure; some of the more prominent have been Bendix, Raytheon, Sylvania, Boeing, and General Electric (which publishes a journal in the area, the *General Electric Defense Quarterly*). This process has an impressive precedent: RAND was originally established as a branch of Douglas Aircraft. The rise of issues of nuclear strategy and disarmament in politics has meant that political action groups have sponsored research in the area. Moreover, our concern with published

3. Lyons and Morton, *Schools for Strategy*, pp. 127–99; Archibald, *Social Conflict*, chap. 3, pp. 29–33, 51–52; Charles V. Kidd, *American Universities and Federal Research* (Cambridge, Mass.: Harvard University Press, Belknap Press, 1959), pp. 175–88.

4. Lyons and Morton, *Schools for Strategy*, pp. 127–99; Archibald, *Social Conflict*, chap. 3, pp. 30–31.

works was expected to include individuals employed by periodicals, of whom the military correspondents are perhaps the most prominent.[5]

Table 22 shows the responses of the sample to Question 7. This question was designed to show how many respondents had been employed full time in work directly related to nuclear strategy and disarmament, as well as the type of institution concerned. Because of this, the question excluded individuals who might have worked for one or more of these institutions without being involved in nuclear strategy and disarmament. It is especially important to note that the group labeled college teachers includes

Table 22

FULL-TIME EMPLOYMENT IN STRATEGY AND DISARMAMENT*

Type of Institution	N	%
College or university (teaching full or part time)	44	19
College or university (no teaching responsibility)	19	8
Research institute affiliated with a college or university	29	13
Private nonprofit research and/or educational institute	64	27
Private corporation (not nonprofit)	16	7
Periodical (privately owned)	18	8
Federal government	36	15
Other (please specify)†	7	3
Total	233	100

* Refers to question "Have you ever been employed full time for over four months by any of the following types of institution, doing work that was directly related to nuclear strategy and disarmament? (Check as many as are applicable.)"

† Of the seven who named other institutions, two named book publishers, and one named each of the following: the Naval War College, the YMCA, a peace organization, a national laboratory, and a religious organization.

5. For a rather inconclusive study of this group, see George V. Underwood, Jr., "The Washington Military Correspondents" (M.A. thesis, University of Wisconsin, 1960).

only those who have worked on strategy and disarmament while teaching rather than all those who have taught. Given the large number of members, it was expected that most of the population would not have worked full time in the area. This was not true; 126, or 66 percent, of the sample named at least one institution. Although the total number was larger than expected, certain other hypotheses were confirmed. Research institutes that were not nonprofit and major industrial corporations were lumped together under the category "private corporation (not nonprofit)" because it was thought that the numbers involved would be too small to allow analysis if they were separated; indeed, the aggregate total was only sixteen. Only one person had been employed full time by a political action group. (Most such activity is probably "extracurricular" work by academics, an area not discussed in this study.)[6] Also as expected, there was a fairly even division between the universities and the research institutes. The research institutes dominated any other single category, with 64 respondents. However, if those at a college or university with and without teaching responsibilities are combined, they total 63. The research institutes affiliated with colleges and universities hold the balance between them.

who goes where?

The central hypothesis of this chapter, again a derivative of the original hypothesis about communities, was that there were four distinct groups among the seven institutional divisions listed in Table 1: universities, research institutes, private corporations, and periodicals. Those who had worked for the federal government were expected to be primarily from the universities and research institutes, and it was not expected that they would form a separate group of their own. The research institutes

6. Archibald, *Social Conflict*, chap. 3, pp. 33–34.

affiliated with a college or university were expected to be closer to universities than the private nonprofit research institutes.

It was expected that those at universities would have the highest proportion of graduate degrees, followed by the private research institutes, private corporations, and periodicals, in that order. Table 23 supports this hypothesis. On this indicator the research institutes affiliated with colleges and universities are more like the nonprofit research institutes than the universities, although they do occupy an intermediate position.

Table 23

EDUCATION AND EMPLOYMENT

	N	Ph.D.	B.A. Only	Signif- icance Level*
College or university teaching full or part time)	44	82%	11%	.001
College or university (no teaching respon- sibility)	19	74	16	.10
Federal government	36	56	17	.15
Research institute affiliated with a college or university	29	55	21	NS
Private nonprofit research and/or educational institute	64	48	23	NS
Private corporation (not nonprofit)	16	25	19	.15
Periodical (privately owned)	18	6	56	.01

* Unless otherwise specified, the significance figures in this chapter refer to a universe of the 126 individuals who had been employed full time for over four months by any of the eight types of institutions doing work directly related to nuclear strategy and disarmament (see Table 22), rather than to the sample of 191.

It was expected that the proportion of perceived influentials at the various institutions would follow a pattern similar to that of graduate degrees. Table 24 suggests that although this is generally true, the differences are in fact artifacts of the educational differences already noted rather than independent.

Table 24

EMPLOYMENT AND PERCEIVED INFLUENTIALS

Institution	Perceived Influentials			Ph.D.'s Who Are Perceived Influentials		
	N	%	Signif-icance Level	N	%	Signif-icance Level
College or university (teach-ing full or part time).......	44	39	.01	36	33	NS
College or university (no teaching responsibility)....	19	37	.20	14	43	NS
Research institute affiliated with college or university...	29	35	.20	16	38	NS
Private nonprofit research and/or educational insti-tute...................	63	30	.10	30	37	NS
Periodical (privately owned)..	18	6	.30	1	0	NS
Federal government.........	36	28	.60	20	35	NS
Private corporation (not non-profit).................	16	0	.05	4	0	NS

motivation

It was expected that respondents who had worked for different institutions would have had different motives for entering the field. In a study using a smaller sample and more intensive inter-views, Kathleen Archibald found a clear relationship.

Interviewees in different organizational settings gave different reasons for starting to work on problems of international conflict. Those in university settings saw themselves as becoming involved initially be-cause of concern about the state of the world—in particular, the like-lihood of nuclear war. . . . Those who had been working in a non-profit research corporation, on the other hand, tended to report that the intellectual challenge initially caught their interest. . . . Over time, concern increases among the non-profit group and intellectual interest gains in salience for the university group. Thus both end up reporting a rather similar interest in influencing policy to improve the state of the world as a dominant objective. That intellectual interests are not given so much weight as a reason for continuing to work in the area does not indicate that they are absent, but merely that they are also present in other areas open to the expert.[7]

Table 25 does not confirm this hypothesis. Although those in university teaching positions were significantly more influenced by a desire to "significantly alter American foreign policy," the differences on the other policy motives, including "concern about the threat of modern weapons to the human race" are not significant. Indeed, of the six policy motives, the research institute respondents had *higher* percentages on two; on three there was no difference, and only on the general motive of altering American foreign policy did the expected greater policy interest of the academics appear. There was also no significant difference on the intellectual motive.

Indeed, the most obvious conclusion to be drawn from Table 25 is that differences in motivation between individuals employed by different institutions are unimportant. As we might expect, those who had taught in colleges and universities were more influenced by the desire to teach and disseminate knowledge and to influence young minds; in regard to the former motive, those at the nonprofit research institutes were significantly *less* motivated than the rest of the group. One unexpected finding was that those who had worked for periodicals had been more influenced by antiwar motives; the difference was significant on the "desire to encourage world disarmament" and notable on "concern about the threat of modern weapons to the human race." The frustration index figure on the former motive among those who had worked for periodicals was a startling 80 percent, although

7. *Social Conflict*, chap. 6, pp. 4–5.

Table 25

MOTIVE AND EMPLOYMENT

	N	%	Signif-icance Level	Frustration Index	
				N	%
Desire to significantly alter American foreign policy					
University (teaching)............	39	31	.01	19	21
University (no teaching).........	15	13	.15	10	20
University research institute.....	24	21	.20	10	0
Private research institute........	58	28	NS	24	17
Private corporation.............	15	40	NS	11	21
Periodical (privately owned)......	13	23	NS	6	17
Federal government............	31	32	NS	18	33
Desire to encourage world disarmament					
University (teaching)............	39	20	NS	12	17
University (no teaching).........	16	19	NS	8	25
University research institute.....	24	17	.20	9	11
Private research institute........	56	20	.20	23	22
Private corporation.............	55	33	NS	11	27
Periodical (privately owned)......	12	33	.05	5	80
Federal government............	30	17	.20	12	8
Concern about moral problems of current American military policy					
University (teaching)............	40	22	NS	10	10
University (no teaching).........	16	25	NS	8	25
University research institute.....	23	26	NS	7	0
Private research institute........	52	25	NS	16	13
Private corporation.............	14	29	NS	7	43
Periodical (privately owned).....	12	25	NS	4	25
Federal government............	26	19	NS	7	43
Concern about threat of modern weapons to human race					
University (teaching)............	40	55	NS	18	44
University (no teaching).........	16	44	NS	9	44
University research institute.....	24	54	NS	13	31
Private research institute........	58	59	NS	28	32
Private corporation.............	15	60	NS	12	25
Periodical (privately owned)......	13	61	.20	5	60
Federal government............	29	62	NS	16	56
Desire to combat world communism					
University (teaching)............	38	18	NS	10	30
University (no teaching).........	16	12	.20	8	25
University research institute.....	24	17	.10	9	22
Private research institute........	55	18	NS	18	22
Private corporation.............	15	13	NS	7	14
Periodical (privately owned)......	12	17	NS	2	0
Federal government............	27	30	.001	12	17

Table 25 —*Continued*

	N	%	Signif-icance Level	Frustration Index	
				N	%
Desire to teach and disseminate knowledge in area					
University (teaching)............	41	46	.01	30	10
University (no teaching).........	16	31	NS	13	8
University research institute.....	25	44	NS	15	13
Private research institute........	55	29	.05	24	4
Private corporation.............	15	33	NS	10	10
Periodical (privately owned)......	15	40	NS	8	13
Federal government............	26	31	NS	15	7
Desire to influence young minds					
University (teaching)............	39	20	.01	16	6
University (no teaching).........	16	19	NS	8	25
University research institute.....	24	12	NS	8	0
Private research institute........	53	13	NS	18	0
Private corporation.............	15	20	NS	7	29
Periodical (privately owned)......	13	23	NS	3	33
Federal government............	26	23	NS	12	8
Intellectual interest in inter-national security affairs					
University (teaching)............	39	79	NS	27	0
University (no teaching).........	16	69	NS	12	8
University research institute.....	25	80	NS	19	0
Private research institute........	58	76	NS	36	8
Private corporation.............	15	60	NS	12	8
Periodical (privately owned)......	14	86	NS	9	0
Federal government............	29	79	NS	20	0
Desire to promote democracy throughout world					
University (teaching)............	39	5	NS	11	9
University (no teaching).........	16	12	NS	9	11
University research institute.....	24	8	NS	8	0
Private research institute........	53	11	NS	16	19
Private corporation.............	14	14	NS	6	0
Periodical (privately owned)......	10	0	NS	4	0
Federal government............	27	11	NS	7	0

the *N* is only five. I was therefore interested to see if this differ-ence was reflected in policy attitudes.

It had not been expected that the motives of those who had been employed by the federal government would differ significantly from those of the rest of the sample; though this was generally true, they were more concerned about the threat of world communism. We have already noted that concern about this threat seemed surprisingly small as a motive;[8] since the rest of the sample is no less interested in altering American foreign policy, this suggests that anticommunism may be helpful in obtaining a government position or, alternatively, that such a position may engender anticommunism. This hypothesis, among others, will be examined in the next section.

policy attitudes

The data do not substantiate a linkage between government service and anticommunism; the attitudes of those who had been employed by the government did not differ significantly from those of the remainder of the sample on any of the eleven policy questions. The same was true of those who had worked for periodicals.

Indeed, of the 77 relationships generated by combining eleven policy questions and seven types of institutions, only one was significant at the .05 level or higher. Since a .05 significance level means one chance in twenty at random, we can safely dismiss this finding. As in the case of motives for entering the field, policy attitudes do not seem to differ significantly among respondents who have been employed by the various types of institutions.

periodicals

The role of periodicals as agents of communication is obviously significant; indeed, a persuasive classification of schools of thought in this area is made in terms of "communication networks" and stresses the role of certain journals.[9] Because of the

8. See above, pp. 55–56.
9. Archibald, *Social Conflict*, chap. 3, pp. 43–44.

importance of this subject, a full page of the questionnaire was devoted to it. Question 30 read:

Opposite each periodical listed below, please indicate about how often you usually read its articles on the subject of strategy and disarmament.

Forty-three periodicals were listed in alphabetical order. They were chosen on the basis of having carried significant articles in the area, a choice facilitated by the construction of the master bibliography of 6,000 items used to select the population;[10] some effort was also made to include as many different types of journals as possible. Newspapers were excluded. Opposite each title was a five-point scale: "not familiar with periodical," "read only occasional articles," "read less than half the articles on this topic," and "read more than half the articles on this topic," as well as "don't know." All other responses given by more than one individual were also coded; of the twenty-five, only one was listed by more than ten respondents, *Survival* (the journal of the Institute of Strategic Studies, London), which had been excluded from the original list because it was British.

A factor analysis was performed on the results of the forty-four periodicals.[11] Eight factors were rotated; together they accounted for 66 percent of the variance. Table 26 shows the periodicals that loaded highly on each of the eight factors, which are listed in descending order of the variance each accounted for. The names of the factors have been invented by the author on the basis of journals loading highly on each; they have no other significance or validity.

10. For a discussion of this process see above, p. 13, and Appendix A.

11. Strictly speaking, factor analysis was not an appropriate statistical technique, since the data were ordinal rather than interval. However, it was felt that the benefits of reducing 44 variables to 8 factors justified the risks. The program used was Yale Computer Center's No. 6S, using the principal axis method and varimax rotation of factors with eigenvalues equal to, or greater than, one.

Table 26

FACTOR LOADINGS OF PERIODICALS AND JOURNALS READ

	Factor Loadings*
Military (17% of variance)	
Army	.87
Journal of the Armed Forces	.80
Air Force/Space Digest	.79
Air University Review	.79
United States Naval Institute Proceedings	.79
Aviation Week	.77
Missiles and Rockets	.76
Military Review	.75
Marine Corps Gazette	.74
Military Affairs	.66
Navy	.62
Social Science (13% of variance)	
International Organization	.83
International Conciliation	.81
American Journal of International Law	.74
American Political Science Review	.73
World Politics	.70
Journal of Conflict Resolution	.66
Annals of the American Academy of Political and Social Science	.53
Daedalus	.51
Foreign Affairs	.50
Orbis	.50
Attentive public (11% of variance)	
Atlantic Monthly	.72
Scientific American	.71
Harper's	.70
Bulletin of the Atomic Scientists	.67
New Republic	.62
Saturday Review	.60
Daedalus	.58
War/Peace Report	.53
Protestant (7% of variance)	
Fellowship	.79
Christian Century	.71
Worldview	.59
Intercom	.56

* In the first five factors, periodicals with factor scores equal to, or larger than, .5 are included; in the last three, the cutting point is shifted to .3.

Table 26 —*Continued*

	Factor Loadings*
Catholic and Jewish (6% of variance)	
America	.76
Commonwealth	.64
Commentary	.57
History (5% of variance)	
American Historical Review	.69
Annals of the American Academy of Political and Social Science	.47
Military Affairs	.46
Virginia Quarterly Review	.43
American Political Science Review	.41
Current History	.39
Atlantic Monthly	.34
Operations research (4% of variance)	
Operations Research	.63
Stanford Research Institute	.39
Military Affairs	.31
Journal of Conflict Resolution	.30
Survival (4% of variance)	
Survival (London)	.84
World Politics	.35
Orbis	.32
Reporter	.31

Kathleen Archibald distinguishes five sources of "Contributors to the War/Peace Discourse": "traditional" work in international law, diplomatic history, and traditional political science; social science; policy research and analysis; physical science; and the peace movement. She sees social science as divided between peace research and conflict research; physical science is divided between those working in and for the government and those primarily concerned about the threat of nuclear weapons.

Several journals are mentioned in connection with this typology. *Foreign Affairs* is seen as the main outlet of the "traditional" group; the *Journal of Conflict Resolution* is regarded as the product of both branches of "social science"; *Bulletin of the Atom-*

ic Scientists is a product of physical scientists concerned about the threat of nuclear weapons; and *War/Peace Report* draws from peace research, policy research and analysis, concerned physical scientists, and the peace movement.[12]

This is a persuasive typology of the *outlets* of the respective groups, but the analysis in this study suggests that it is not reflected in the *reading habits* of the private nuclear strategists. Thus *Foreign Affairs* and *Journal of Conflict Resolution* load on the same factor. *Bulletin of the Atomic Scientists*, judging from the company it keeps, is reaching a wider audience than physical scientists, as of course it was designed to do. *War/Peace Report* does seem to play the role attributed to it as a link between various schools of thought, although this is not shown in Table 27; aside from its loading on the attentive public factor, other loadings are: social science .41, Protestant .32, history .25, and operations research .11. However, it suffers the handicap of a *negative* loading on the largest factor, –.17 on military.

Foreign Affairs seems to be in a better position to connect the various factors; its loadings, aside from that on social science, are: military .26, attentive public .36, Catholic-Jewish .15, history .18, operations research .17, and *Survival* .24, thus loading above .1 on seven of eight factors, excluding only the Protestant one. *Current History* is another candidate; aside from its loading on the history factor, its loadings are: military .18, social science .28, attentive public .28, Protestant .29, Catholic-Jewish .32, operations research .17, and *Survival* .20, loading over .1 on all eight factors.

Factor scores of respondents were used as an index of periodicals; Table 27 examines the relationship between periodicals and employment. The largest difference between college teachers and those working for research institutes is the former's much greater interest in the social science group of periodicals. This may reflect the general preeminence of physical scientists at research insti-

---

12. *Social Conflict*, chap. 3, pp. 43–44.

Table 27

EMPLOYMENT AND PERIODICALS

	% of Scores above 1.0	N	Signif-icance Level
Military			
University (teaching).................	7	44	NS
University (no teaching)..............	11	19	NS
University research institute...........	3	29	NS
Private research institute.............	8	64	NS
Private corporation...................	0	16	NS
Periodical (privately owned)..........	6	18	NS
Federal government.................	8	36	NS
Social Science			
University (teaching).................	41	44	.001
University (no teaching)..............	47	19	.01
University research institute...........	38	29	.01
Private research institute.............	16	64	NS
Private corporation...................	19	16	NS
Periodical (privately owned)..........	0	18	.08
Federal government.................	22	36	NS
Attentive public			
University (teaching).................	9	44	NS
University (no teaching)..............	5	19	NS
University research institute...........	10	29	NS
Private research institute.............	14	64	NS
Private corporation...................	13	16	NS
Periodical (privately owned)..........	11	18	NS
Federal government.................	11	36	NS
Protestant			
University (teaching).................	5	44	NS
University (no teaching)..............	5	19	NS
University research institute...........	7	29	NS
Private research institute.............	11	64	NS
Private corporation...................	19	16	.20
Periodical (privately owned)..........	0	18	.10
Federal government.................	11	36	NS
Catholic and Jewish			
University (teaching).................	11	44	NS
University (no teaching)..............	5	19	NS
University research institute...........	14	29	NS
Private research institute.............	9	64	.10
Private corporation...................	6	16	NS
Periodical (privately owned)..........	11	18	.20
Federal government.................	17	36	.15

Table 27 *—Continued*

	% of Scores above 1.0	N	Signif-icance Level
History			
University (teaching)	11	44	NS
University (no teaching)	5	19	.15
University research institute	7	29	NS
Private research institute	9	64	NS
Private corporation	6	16	NS
Periodical (privately owned)	6	18	NS
Federal government	8	36	NS
Operations research			
University (teaching)	11	44	NS
University (no teaching)	5	19	NS
University research institute	10	29	NS
Private research institute	9	64	NS
Private corporation	12	16	.08
Periodical (privately owned)	17	18	NS
Federal government	14	36	NS
Survival			
University (teaching)	14	44	NS
University (no teaching)	11	19	NS
University research institute	14	29	NS
Private research institute	14	64	NS
Private corporation	6	16	NS
Periodical (privately owned)	6	18	NS
Federal government	11	36	NS

tutes;[13] however, considering the pride of these institutes in their success in interdisciplinary work, it is rather surprising to see their low scores on a factor that includes the major professional journals in political science, international relations, international law, and general social science. Interestingly, there is little difference between research institutes and the college teachers on the operations research factor, where the research institutes might have been expected to have more interest. All in all, with the notable exception of the social science factor, we are again struck with the similarities rather than the differences between

13. Smith, *RAND Corporation*, pp. 60–65.

these two groups. It is not possible to identify the factors with the institutions employing individuals in the area.

employment mobility

If the hypotheses about the distinct nature of various institutions were correct, we would expect that mobility between them would be relatively low. (For the purpose of this section, the seven individuals who had indicated an institution other than those listed were lumped together as "other.") There was in fact a good deal of mobility among those institutions. Of the 126 individuals who had been employed by one or more of them, 60 (47 percent) named only one, 39 (31 percent) named two, 17 (13 percent) named three, 7 (6 percent) named four, 2 (2 percent) named five, and one well-traveled individual named six. Thus of those who had worked for at least one institution, over half had worked for more than one type.

These 8 types of institutions gave 28 theoretically possible pairs. Only 2 of these 28 had no respondents, another indication of the high mobility in the area. For each pair a mobility percentage P was computed with the formula $P = B/(T - B)$ when B is the number of individuals who have been employed by both institutions in question and T is the total number of individuals who have worked for each of the institutions. The P figures ranged from 0 percent in two cases to a maximum of 30 percent; 14 of the pairs had P figures between 1 percent and 10 percent, 8 were between 11 percent and 20 percent, and 4 were between 21 percent and 30 percent. These four pairs with their P figures and Ns (in this case $N = T - B$) were: university (teaching)-university research institute (30 percent, 56), university (teaching)-private nonprofit research institute (24 percent, 87), and university (teaching)-federal government (23 percent, 65).

As a crude indicator of the mobility of individuals who had worked for each of the eight types of institutions, a mobility index was constructed by adding the P figures for the seven pairs of each institution. Although this index is the sum of percentages, it is not a percentage of anything; it has no meaning except as an index in comparison with those of other institutions. The mobility index figures for the eight institutions are given in Table 28. They suggest that individuals associated with universities have more mobility than the remainder of the sample. However, a good deal of this may be due to mobility within the three categories that

Table 28

**MOBILITY INDEX FIGURES FOR
EIGHT TYPES OF INSTITUTIONS**

Type of Institution	Mobility Index
College or university (teaching)	116
University research institute	109
College or university (no teaching)	92
Federal government	91
Private nonprofit research institute	79
Private corporation (not nonprofit)	45
Periodical (privately owned)	28
Other	24

are related to the university. In any event, the large break in Table 28 is between the nonprofit research institutes and private corporations. The difference between the research institutes and the universities remains significant, but it is not large enough to confirm the hypothesis with the decisiveness desired. The separation of those employed by private corporations and especially those working for periodicals from the remainder of the sample is graphically revealed in the table.

Since the position of research institutes affiliated with a college or university was of especial interest, Table 29 gives the P figures for the seven pairs related to this institution. It suggests that its personnel have closer ties to the universities than the private research institutes but that the latter connection nevertheless remains substantial.

Although these figures are interesting, it should be noted that they are no more than suggestive. There simply were not enough

Table 29

P FIGURES FOR UNIVERSITY RESEARCH INSTITUTES

Institution	P	#	N (B - T)
College or university (teaching)	30%	17	56
College or university (no teaching)	20	8	40
Private nonprofit research institute	18	14	79
Private corporation (not nonprofit)	15	6	39
Federal government	14	8	57
Periodical (privately owned)	6	3	44
Other	5	2	34

data to answer the questions about mobility with confidence. Real interest was in the probability of a given individual working for a particular institution accepting a position at any of the eight types of institutions when he changed his job, including the same type as that which he was leaving. This would require having data on changes *within* each institutional category as well as *between* them. Without such information, it is really impossible to evaluate the P figures other than by comparison with other P figures. For instance, does the 30 percent P figure between college teaching and college research institutes mean that mobility is high or not? To answer this, we would need to know what the mobility rate is within each category; the 30 percent may represent every individual who has changed positions, or it may involve only a small fraction of the total movement.

Much of the polemical discussion concerning the private nuclear strategists has centered around the impact of government sponsorship upon research in strategy. The classic case has been the research institute, which is almost totally dependent upon such support. The university, on the other hand, has been assumed to be more independent, at least as an institution, although individual members might also be on the government research payroll. This chapter suggests that this apparent difference in financial support is not reflected in differences in either motivation or policy attitudes. It may be, of course, that everyone working in the field has been tainted, regardless of his sponsorship; at any rate there seems no particular reason for those in universities to regard their opposite numbers in research institutes as being significantly more subservient to government. The field of study, rather than the employing institution, seems the more important factor in determining the outlook of an individual.

strategy and the academic disciplines

One obvious initial step in dealing with a new intellectual problem is to bring to bear on it the relevant knowledge already available. This in turn involves some classification of the problem in order to determine just what knowledge is relevant, what sort of expertise is appropriate. Much of this knowledge and expertise has been cataloged in terms of academic disciplines. This is true not only for individuals working in universities but also for those whose higher education has been shaped by the structure of the disciplines.

Academic disciplines are among that large category of human institutions that are easier to illustrate than define; most of the discussion as to the form, function, and scope of a given discipline appears to be an attempt to impose a logical framework upon a historical phenomenon not particularly amenable to such structuring.[1] This very attempt, however, suggests that the dis-

1. For a graphic illustration of this in one discipline, see Vernon Van Dyke, "The Optimum Scope of Political Science," and the accompanying

ciplines do serve some useful purpose. Given the explosion of human knowledge, there is an obvious need for some form of division of labor. Indeed, the modern problem is not so much whether the disciplines should continue to exist but whether they can develop sufficient unity to keep their component specialties together; in many cases it is this threat of further fissioning that has caused renewed concern about the philosophical and logical bases of the disciplines.

Another indication of the utility of disciplines has been their adoption by the research institutes, which are dedicated to the ideal of interdisciplinary work; the most obvious example is at RAND, where departments have been formed on the basis of disciplines, and where problems are tackled by committees made up of representatives from the relevant departments.[2] All in all, despite the criticisms it has endured, the institution of the academic discipline seems likely to continue into the foreseeable future.

One result of the lack of a sociology of academe is that we have very little solid evidence of differences among students trained in different disciplines.[3] Nevertheless, the common assumption that such differences do exist and are meaningful is a reasonable one. Academic training, especially on the graduate level, centers around the department, which in most schools is almost autonomous. If the student goes into academics, he is hired by the same sort of department, presumably continuing the same socialization process. It seems likely that this process will affect the organizations to which he belongs, the journals he regularly reads, the individuals whose opinions he solicits and respects, the problems he studies, his techniques of research, and the authori-

---

commentary and discussion in James C. Charlesworth, ed., *A Design for Political Science: Scope, Objectives, and Methods*, American Academy of Political and Social Science, Monograph 6 (Philadelphia, 1966), pp. 1–62; see especially the remarks by Louis Hartz, pp. 24–27, 45–46, 48–50, 57–58.

2. Smith, *RAND Corporation*, pp. 148–52, 165–82.

3. For a "modest proposal" to remedy this situation, see Somit and Tanenhaus, *American Political Science*, pp. 164–68.

ties he cites.[4] This reasoning was at least persuasive enough to hypothesize that differences would appear in the sample among those with different disciplinary affiliations; as we shall see, this expectation was borne out by the data.

There were two questions relating to the discipline of the respondent. The first simply asked in what field he took his highest degree; the second asked whether he was affiliated with a discipline and, if so, what it was. The first had the advantage of a large N (177, or 92 percent of the sample); the second had an N of 115, since 62 respondents said that they were not affiliated with a discipline. If nearly all who answered both questions had given the same answers, the first question would probably have been used with confidence. However, only 61 percent of those who answered both questions did give the same answer (N was 112). Since interest was in the effects of a discipline rather than academic background per se, it was decided to work with the second question, even though the N was only 115, or 60 percent of the sample.

the dominance of political science

One of the most interesting aspects of nuclear strategy and disarmament is the remarkable number of disciplines and professions that can make a convincing claim to relevance at some level. The stress on technology makes nearly all of the physical sciences relevant; aside from the obvious example of nuclear physics, there are the more unlikely areas, such as seismic geology in detecting nuclear tests or genetics in determining the effects of radioactive fallout. Every social science can be plausibly invoked in the study of war and conflict, as well as some of the major humanities, such

---

4. It is difficult to explain convincingly the "culture shock" that an individual trained in a particular discipline may experience when discussing a subject of mutual interest with a person from another field, the lack of common knowledge and assumptions that may be revealed, as well as the more subtle differences of perspective.

as history. Philosophy and ethics have something to say on the morality of war in general and nuclear weapons in particular. The professions of law, theology, medicine, and journalism, not to mention the military, cannot be excluded out of hand. Though all of these may not provide automatic entry into our population, they all do give sufficient "handle" to bring in anyone seriously interested without undue intellectual convolutions.

Aside from the possible relevance of a whole spectrum of intellectual backgrounds, there have been relatively few standards that an interested newcomer to the field must achieve before being admitted. This is especially true in the manner in which our population was selected; by including such a variety of publications, it made it difficult for any particular group of individuals to block all the possible outlets of ideas. (We will consider the question of the existence of an establishment in the next chapter, under the rubric of professionalization.) Moreover, there has been a good deal of emphasis on interdisciplinary work in this area, both in the universities and the research institutes.

Given both relevance and access, it was expected that several disciplines would dominate the area. This expectation was shared by respondents who were interviewed. It was further heightened by the discussions of contributions of various disciplines. The role of economics, for instance, has been regarded as quite important by many observers, both in cost-effectiveness studies and in the wider application of certain aspects of economic theory and game theory to deterrence theory. Bernard Brodie, himself one of the best-known private strategists and a political scientist, has remarked:

Most of those who have made their mark today as theorists in strategy have been trained as economists, or at least have more than a bowing acquaintance with the concepts and principles in that field.[5]

The role of the physical scientists in strategy and disarmament

5. Brodie, "The Scientific Strategists," p. 247; see also his "The McNamara Phenomenon," p. 679.

has been great enough to produce at least two major studies of the phenomenon,[6] and such names as Linus Pauling, Hans Bethe, and Edward Teller have been in the forefront of public debate on the subject. Psychology and psychiatry have also been conspicuous contributors, so much so that Kathleen Archibald, a sociologist, can say:

> Sociology and political science, the two social science disciplines seemingly most relevant to problems of war and peace, have contributed less to the discourse than psychology or economics.[7]

Gene Lyons and Louis Morton (a political scientist and a historian) suggest that political science is also important:

> The study of military affairs has never been fully accepted as an important professional concern by historians. Political scientists have been the most receptive to national security studies, both because international relations has developed as a major field within the discipline and because of the political scientist's concern with the impact of national security measures on democratic institutions. Few sociologists, on the other hand, have shown interest in the implications of national security for changes in the social order. The contribution of economists has been uneven and is difficult to generalize about. As a group, economists tend to regard national security as an area of practical application of economic theory, like labor or agricultural economics, yet have not given the field comparable attention. Nevertheless, a few economists, especially those of the RAND Corporation, have applied the techniques of economic analysis to the study of strategic alternatives with great success.[8]

In view of this evidence, perhaps the most startling, as well as the most obvious, conclusion from the data is the overwhelming

6. Gilpin, *American Scientists and Nuclear Weapons Policy*, and A. Smith, *Peril and a Hope;* see also Schilling, "Scientists, Foreign Policy, and Politics" and Wohlstetter, "Strategy and the Natural Sciences," in Gilpin and Wright, *Scientists and National Policy-Making*.

7. Kathleen Archibald, "Social Science Approaches to Peace: Problems and Issues," *Social Problems* 11 (1963), 98.

8. Lyons and Morton, *Schools for Strategy*, p. 51.

dominance of political science on practically all the indicators over any other discipline or obvious group of disciplines. This dominance appears first in sheer numbers, as shown in Table 30. Indeed, it is so great that in order to get Ns of reasonable size, disciplines had to be combined, as shown in the lower part of the table.

The amalgamation was something of a problem. Putting the physical sciences together seemed obvious. Grouping the social sciences other than political science together was more controversial. In practice this meant grouping economics, psychology, and sociology, excluding history. This was done primarily on the basis that the three social sciences share a "scientific" approach, a desire for quantifiable data, and a taste for mathematical models and theory, as opposed to history, especially the subdivision of military history. (On these grounds political science would have constituted a difficult marginal case between these poles; probably it should have been divided into two groups along the lines of the behavioral-traditional split.[9] However, its dominance allowed us to avoid this dilemma.)

Beyond this, the problems mount, in both logical combinations and sample size. Aside from being quite small, the humanities group is made up of history and philosophy in unequal proportions, with a respondent in English thrown in for good measure. The professions are almost evenly divided between law and theology. These combinations may make sense in a college catalog, but there seems to be no particular justification for combining them in this context. A better case could be made for linking history with law and philosophy with theology. The Ns remain at 9, however, and there seems little sense in combining them all into a residual category. Therefore, we shall be concerned with four groups: political science, physical sciences, other social sciences, and those not affiliated with an academic discipline.

Although it was decided not to use the results of the question

9. For an interesting empirical demonstration of the existence of this division, see Somit and Tanenhaus, *American Political Science*, pp. 21–24.

Table 30

DISCIPLINARY AFFILIATIONS OF THE SAMPLE

Discipline	N	%
Not affiliated with an academic discipline...................	62	35
Political science..	53	30
Physics...	10	6
Economics..	7	3
History...	6	3
Psychology...	6	3
Sociology...	6	3
Law..	5	2
Theology...	4	2
Philosophy..	3	2
Engineering...	2	1
Mathematics..	2	1
Military and/or naval science............................	2	1
Physical science (general or other).......................	2	1
Business administration.................................	1	1
Chemistry..	1	1
English...	1	1
Geography..	1	1
International relations..................................	1	1
Physiology..	1	1
Speech...	1	1
Total...	177	100
Not affiliated with an academic discipline...................	62	35
Political science..	53	30
Physical sciences......................................	18	10
Social sciences (other than political science)..............	19	11
Miscellaneous...	25	14
Total...	177	100

about the field of the respondent's degree in determining his disciplinary affiliation, it is perhaps worth noting that again political science dominated the other disciplines. Only 19 percent of the sample took their degrees in political science. However, another 11 percent took theirs in international relations, and comparison between the two questions on disciplines showed that nearly all of these individuals gave their discipline as political science; none of them said that they were affiliated with international relations as distinguished from political science.

(The one man who was so identified took his degree in law.) It therefore seemed logical to regard international relations as a subdivision of political science; when the two were combined, they accounted for 30 percent of the sample, as compared with 20 percent for the professions, 18 percent for physical sciences, and 24 percent for the other social sciences.

Table 31 reveals the extent of the domination of political science. On the thirteen indicators examined, the percentage of political science drops below its percentage of the sample as a

Table 31

DISCIPLINES AND INDICATORS OF INFLUENCE AND STATUS

	N	Political Science	Physical Sciences	Other Social Sciences	Not Affiliated with an Academic Discipline	Significance Level
Sample...............................	177	30%	10%	11%	35%*	†
Perceived influentials						
Total (all named by one or more respondents other than themselves).........	34	44	12	24	12	.01
Highly influential (all named by five or more respondents)...............	9	33	11	33	11	.02
Publication point scores over 15..........	25	32	4	8	44	NS
Worked on government research contract in strategy and disarmament............	81	53	7	11	15	.001
Specializing in area within strategy and disarmament......................	28	71	0	11	†	.05
Employment by institution						
College or university (teaching).........	41	71	2	15	2	.001
College or university (no teaching)......	17	76	0	6	6	.01
University research institute............	28	78	4	4	7	.001
Private nonprofit research institute......	59	41	7	12	32	NS
Private corporation (not nonprofit).......	16	31	6	6	38	NS
Periodical (privately owned)............	17	6	0	0	94	.001
Federal government.................	34	50	6	0	32	.20

* **Percentage figures total across.**

† **Not applicable.**

Table 32

PROFESSIONAL ORGANIZATIONS IN WHICH
MORE THAN TEN RESPONDENTS CLAIM MEMBERSHIP

Organizations	N	%
American Political Science Association....................	49	29
Institute of Strategic Studies (London).....................	17	10
American Association of University Professors..............	14	8
International Studies Association..........................	13	8
American Association for the Advance of Science...........	11	6
American Physical Society................................	11	6
American Institute of Aeronautics and Astronautics..........	10	6
American Society of International Law.....................	10	6
Council on Foreign Relations.............................	10	6
United States Naval Institute............................	10	6

whole on only one, employment by periodicals; moreover, eight of the twelve differences are statistically significant. Even though political scientists were somewhat oversampled, these differences are impressive. Explanation for the high estimate of the influence of economics may be found in the two measures of perceived influentials; although political science dominates in the total of such individuals, economics competes when we limit consideration to those who were named by four or more respondents. Of the nine individuals so named who answered the question, three were political scientists, two were economists, and one each was a sociologist, physical scientist, lawyer, and nonaffiliated. Since only seven individuals identified themselves as economists, this indicates that nearly a third of them were in this high-status group and that they have clearly had an influence out of proportion to their numbers, substantiating Lyons and Morton. How-

Table 33

DISCIPLINES AND PERCEIVED INFLUENCE OF FIELDS OF STUDY

Discipline	Political Science	Physical Sciences	Other Social Sciences	Not Affiliated with an Academic Discipline	Total Sample	Significance Level
	Respondents' Affiliation					
Political science	78%*	69%	64%	60%	67%	NS
Physical sciences	12	43	33	12	18	.05
Social sciences	78	77	82	63	72	NS
Economics	33	58	60	48	46	NS
Psychology	71	77	71	58	66	NS
Sociology	71	78	85	68	72	NS
Operations research	20	33	0	23	21	.20

* Percentages given are for those who felt that influence of a discipline had been "much too small" or "too small."

ever, this number was insufficient to counterbalance the political scientists in influence even on this indicator, and on others the economists were totally swamped.

The table also suggests that the major competition to political science comes not from the other disciplines but from those not affiliated with a discipline. It was expected that individuals working full time at institutions outside of universities would tend to be disproportionately nonaffiliated, given the interdisciplinary nature of the work done at many of these institutions; this was substantiated, at least to the point that the proportions remained roughly similar to those of the sample, with the notable exception of periodicals. Certainly the private nonprofit research institutes were the major chink in the dominance of the political scientists. This potential influence by the nonaffiliated was not matched by a high proportion of perceived influentials or even of those who have worked on a government research contract, although it may in part account for their high publication point scores.

Table 32 gives another indication of the dominance of political science. Question 15 asked: "To what professional organizations do you belong?" The first five responses were coded. The question was answered by 170 respondents, who listed 130 different organizations. However, only ten organizations were listed by ten or more respondents; they are listed in Table 32. The most obvious aspect of this table is the leading position of the American Political Science Association; it has no competition as the most popular organization. As noted in Appendix C, 19 percent of the nonrespondents were members. The Institute of Strategic Studies, the second organization listed above, is the closest thing to a professional organization in strategy and disarmament that now exists. The International Studies Association attempts to perform a similar function for international relations. Physics is the only other discipline represented in the table; as in Table 30, it takes second place only to political science, if we assume that international relations and political science are connected.

Another indicator of the roles of the various disciplines is the attitudes of respondents toward them. Question 29 read:

Please indicate opposite each field of study whether you believe that *in the past* its general influence in the area of nuclear strategy and disarmament has been too great, too small, or about right.

Table 33 gives the results for certain important disciplines. Because of the nature of the data, it should be read differently from Table 31; the first figure, 78 percent, means that 78 percent of the political scientists felt that political science had had too little influence. Major divisions were expected between respondents affiliated with different disciplines, with each contending that his own had had too little influence; however, this difference was significant only in the physical sciences. There seemed to be general agreement that political science, psychology, and sociology had had too little influence; the difference that Archibald suggests between psychology and the other two disciplines did not seem to be felt by members of the sample. There was also agreement that economics had had too little influence, but the level of concern was much lower, presumably reflecting the idea suggested by Brodie and Archibald that economics had had more influence than the other social sciences.

However, this unity may be deceptive, since it is present where the consensus was that the field had had too little influence. The field that showed high cleavage was also the only one where the sample as a whole asserted that it had had too much influence. Forty-eight percent of the sample said that the physical sciences had had too much influence, but only 21 percent of the physical scientists agreed. A similar pattern emerges, upon closer examination of the data, for operations research. Respondents identified with a particular field seemed unwilling to state that their own area had had too much influence, an interesting display of self-interest.

One of the most interesting implications of Table 33 is that if political science actually dominates the area, it seems to have aroused no opposition from members of other disciplines. We would normally expect, in an area which attracts individuals from many different disciplines, the practitioners of the dominant one to be resented by others. However, there was no significant difference on attitudes toward political science among our disciplinary divisions; equally as important, the respondents agreed that political science actually had had too little influence. Thus one expected internal barrier to the dominance of the area by a single discipline does not seem to exist. It seems likely that this is a factor of the low visibility of this dominance; in personal interviews respondents generally expressed surprise at the findings on this subject.

We have examined three types of material bearing on the relationship between the disciplines and strategy and disarmament: the literature, which generally suggests that several disciplines have made major contributions; questionnaire data showing political science dominating the field; and respondents' opinions that political science, along with sociology and psychology, have made too little contribution to the field, as opposed to physical science and operations research.

It is important to note that these materials are not entirely comparable. To take only the latter two, their results are not necessarily incompatible. In the first place, there is a difference between a discipline—a collection of intellectual material organized around a particular topic—and the people identified with that discipline. The fact that the sample felt that the physical *sciences* had had too much influence does not mean that it will discourage physical *scientists* from working in the field, especially if they are willing to do work outside the physical sciences. Indeed, such work was practically mandatory for inclusion in the population, since admission was based on publications on nuclear weapons policy rather than technical topics such as the mechanics of ballistic missiles.

Brodie illuminates another problem in his observation that those prominent in strategy and disarmament are either economists or have "more than a bowing acquaintance" with the basic principles of the discipline. It would be a mistake to put too much faith on the divisions between disciplines; between actual academic work in different disciplines (11 percent of the sample, after all, took their last degree in international relations, avowedly an interdisciplinary field if separated from political science) and the discussion of various concepts from other fields, it is obvious that a given individual may be reasonably competent in several disciplines, especially if what is required is only a general grasp of basic principles. This is especially likely in a field such as the study of strategy and disarmament, which has stressed interdisciplinary work. However, there was no way of testing this in the questionnaire; thus *economics* may have had a tremendous impact, even though *economists* have not gone into the field in large numbers.

Even if it is assumed that there is some kind of identity between a discipline and its practitioners, the opinions on the past role of the disciplines do not use a common standard. For instance, if it was assumed that political science should dominate the field almost totally, we might look at the data about its present influence and assert that it should have even more of a role. Moreover, if we felt that economics should have less influence than political science, we might say that economics now has too much influence and political science too little, even if the latter has more than the former. Nevertheless, despite these caveats, the numbers and influence of political science suggest that its influence has been grossly underestimated.

If this is true, we must examine the data to see what implications it may have for the development of the field. Three obvious areas of investigation are motivation in entering the area, periodicals read, and policy attitudes; each will be examined in turn. Generally speaking, hypotheses relating to all of these areas were originally formulated for physical scientists; however, although there was some consideration of the relationship between various social science disciplines, hypotheses about differences between political science and the amalgamation of the other social sciences were formulated only after initial analysis revealed that this division would have to be used.

motivations

It was expected that the physical scientists would be motivated primarily by policy concerns centering around the threat of modern weapons to mankind, using the stereotype of the remorseful nuclear physicist as well as writings on the subject. This was a product of a more general hypothesis: that those entering the field could be divided into those motivated by concerns outside of their professional work, who would be primarily interested in policy questions,[10] and those whose work was more closely related to their vocation, who would be more oriented toward academic

---

10. For a persuasive discussion of the problems of part-time involvement in this field, see Archibald, "Social Science Approaches to Peace," pp. 99–100.

Table 34

DISCIPLINES AND MOTIVES FOR ENTERING FIELD

Motive	Political Science	Physical Sciences	Other Social Sciences	Not Affiliated with an Academic Discipline	Significance Level
Desire to significantly alter American foreign policy............	26%*	50%	56%	40%	NS
Desire to encourage world disarmament......................	18	50	39	36	.01
Concern about moral problems of current American military policy..	19	50	18	38	.05
Concern about threat of modern weapons to human race.........	56	72	72	64	NS
Desire to combat world communism.....................	16	8	0	19	.01
Desire to promote democracy throughout world..............	8	8	6	8	.01
Desire to teach and disseminate knowledge in this area..........	47	12	19	28	.15
Intellectual interest in international security affairs.........	84	46	29	63	.001
Desire to influence young minds...	19	20	12	20	NS

* **Percentages given are for those who said motive had "very much" influence oh their decision to enter field.**

motives. The number of political scientists involved, combined with Lyons and Morton's assertion that political science has been the most receptive discipline to the development of national security affairs as a specialty area,[11] suggests that political scien-

11. Lyons and Morton, *Schools for Strategy*, pp. 51–98, especially p. 51.

tists would be more likely to take the latter view, as compared with physical and social scientists.

Table 34 supports these hypotheses. For political scientists the single most important motive was "intellectual interest in international security affairs," whereas for physical scientists and other social scientists it was "concern about the threat of modern weapons to the human race." The difference on the intellectual interest motive was significant at the .001 level. That on the "threat of modern weapons" motive was not significant, probably because of the general agreement on it. However, on a related but more controversial motive, "desire to encourage world disarmament," the physical scientists did have a significantly higher

Table 35

DISCIPLINES AND LOADING ON PERIODICALS FACTORS

Factors	Political Science	Physical Sciences	Other Social Sciences	Not Affiliated with an Academic Discipline	Significance Level
Military (17% of variance).........	8%*	11%	10%	8%	.001
Social and political science (13%)..	49	0	0	0	.001
Attentive public (11%)............	8	40	11	21	.01
Protestant (7%).................	6	22	5	11	NS
Catholic-Jewish (6%).............	15	11	16	13	NS
History (5%)....................	7	18	32	8	.08
Operations research (4%).........	11	6	0	19	NS
Survival (4%)...................	15	0	10	3	.005

* Percentages of group loading over 1.00 on particular factor. Note that factor names are products of the author rather than of the analysis; see Table 26 for their composition.

percentage; a similar pattern appeared on "concern about the moral problems of current American military policy."

One interesting exception to the hypothesis appeared: the political scientists were significantly more motivated by a "desire to combat world communism," supporting the theory advanced by nearly all respondents interviewed that political scientists as a group tend to be more "hard line" (or "realistic," depending on the observer's perspective). However, even 56 percent of the political scientists designated the threat of modern weapons, as opposed to only 16 percent who named anticommunism. Although differences over motives were great enough to support the hypotheses, the patterns of agreement remained impressive; the American Political Science Association is apparently not ready to merge with the John Birch Society.

periodicals

We have already discussed the factor analysis technique applied to the questions relating to what periodicals the respondent read. To recapitulate, forty-two periodicals were listed on the questionnaire in alphabetical order. Each had a five-point scale, indicating approximately what percentage of its articles on strategy and disarmament were read by the respondent. Space was left for others to be added; only one journal, *Survival,* was listed by over ten respondents and thus included in further analysis. A factor analysis on this data yielded eight factors, accounting for 66 percent of the variance; factor loadings of periodicals may be found in Table 26. Table 35 shows how members of the various disciplines loaded on these factors. A good deal of difference between the disciplines was expected, since the periodical factors seemed to be divided along disciplinary lines, as shown in their titles. This was certainly borne out by the data; in five of the eight factors in Table 35 the significance level was over .05, and in three it was over .005. Undoubtedly, the most startling difference was on the factor "social and political science," with half of the political scientists loading over 1.00, whereas no member of the other three groups did so. This factor includes the major journals of political science, international relations, international law, and general social science; it forms the logical outlet for the work of the political scientists, who, we have suggested, hold a dominant position among other disciplines. This suggests that they are largely producing for their own consumption. Generally, the magnitude of these differences was greater than had been hypothesized, although the fact that the factors together accounted for only about two-thirds of the variance in the sample mitigates this conclusion somewhat.

policy attitudes

In his discussion of the policy perspectives "moderately characteristic of many scientists . . . who have participated in national security policy in recent times," Warner Schilling summarizes a good deal of the discussion on the subject of the physical scientists in politics. He sees six perspectives: naïve utopianism or naïve belligerency, the "whole-problem approach," quantum jumps versus improvements, technology for its own sweet sake, the sense of paradise lost, and science serves mankind.[12] Operationalizing these characteristics was something of a problem, and, indeed, for several it could not be done with the data available. However, Table 36 suggests some data relevant to "naïve utopianism or naïve belligerency," "the whole problem approach," and "quantum jumps versus improvements." All of these suggest a tendency to go to extremes on policy questions. Table 36 takes the responses to a series of questions on policy attitudes, mostly related to world communism, which were answered on a seven-

12. Schilling, "Scientists, Foreign Policy, and Politics," pp. 152–63; see also the other works named in footnote 2 above.

Table 36

DISCIPLINES AND EXTREME POLICY ATTITUDES

Policy Statement	Political Science	Physical Sciences	Other Social Sciences	Not Affiliated with an Academic Discipline	Significance Level
American foreign policy since World War II has not faced up to the fundamental problem of a hostile Communist foe dedicated to its destruction....................	65%*	56%	78%	62%	NS
American foreign policy since World War II has placed too much emphasis on the threat of world communism and the Soviet bloc.....	29	56	61	49	.08
The aggressive tendencies of the Soviet Union have been greatly reduced since World War II......	15	50	42	29	.02
In ten years China will be a greater threat to the United States than the Soviet Union will be.........	20	39	23	40	NS
It seems likely that, within this century, the Soviet Union and the United States will be allied against China.......................	15	7	0	13	NS
The present system of deterrence seems unlikely to last until the end of the century without breaking down in a central nuclear war........................	45	50	38	35	NS
In a nuclear age, the American government must regard itself as being responsible, not only to the American people, but also to the people of the world.............	35	71	74	63	.005

* **Percentages of each group giving one of two extreme responses on a seven-point agree-disagree statement.**

Table 36 —*Continued*

Policy Statement	Political Science	Physical Sciences	Other Social Sciences	Not Affiliated with an Academic Discipline	Significance Level
The American policy of a containment of the Soviet Union has been a success	27	19	40	30	NS
Some form of world government is the only long-term solution to the problem of the destructiveness of modern weapons and opposing nationalisms	21	60	56	54	.005
The military should have a greater voice in strategic decisions than it has today	46	69	74	55	NS
Index of extremism	318	477	486	430	

point agree-disagree scale; it gives the percentage of each disciplinary group that chose one of the two extreme responses.[13]

Of the ten attitudes listed, social scientists had the largest percentage of extreme responses on five, physical scientists on four, and political scientists on one. Only three of the ten had significance figures over .05, and in one of these the social scientists had the highest percentage. A crude index of extremism may be constructed by simply adding the percentages for each disciplinary group; it groups the physical and social scientists against the political scientists, with the nonaffiliated in the middle but closer to the physical and social scientists. There is some support for

13. I am indebted to Robert Axelrod for this idea.

Table 37

DISCIPLINES AND DIRECTION OF POLICY ATTITUDES

Policy Statement	Percentage Agreeing with Statement				Significance Level
	Political Science	Physical Sciences	Other Social Sciences	Not Affiliated with an Academic Discipline	
American foreign policy since World War II has not faced up to the fundamental problem of a hostile Communist foe dedicated to its destruction....................	6	0	0	19	.03
American foreign policy since World War II has placed too much emphasis on the threat of world communism and the Soviet bloc.....	60	87	94	56	.05
The aggressive tendencies of the Soviet Union have been greatly reduced since World War II......	76	81	95	71	NS
In ten years China will be a greater threat to the United States than the Soviet Union will be.........	41	54	54	60	NS
It seems likely that, within this century, the Soviet Union and the United States will be allied against China........................	37	86	46	51	.02
The major threat to American national interests abroad since World War II has been Russian and Chinese national power rather than Communist ideology.......	17	21	15	20	NS
The present system of deterrence seems unlikely to last until the end of the century without breaking down in a central nuclear war........................	37	42	75	49	NS

Table 37 —*Continued*

Policy Statement	Percentage Agreeing with Statement				
	Political Science	Physical Sciences	Other Social Sciences	Not Affiliated with an Academic Discipline	Significance Level
The American policy of containment of the Soviet Union has been a success.	75	62	73	71	NS
Percentage that has publicly disagreed with a U.S. government position on strategy and disarmament.	88	83	88	86	NS
In a nuclear age the American government must regard itself as being responsible, not only to the American people, but also to the people of the world.	96	100	95	86	NS
Some form of world government is the only long-term solution to the problem of the destruciveness of modern weapons and opposing nationalisms.	43	80	85	65	.05
The military should have a greater voice in strategic decisions than it has today.	14	6	5	33	.03
Military and naval science have had too much influence in strategy and disarmament in the past.	43	43	85	46	.08

the hypothesis, although a case could be made for rephrasing it to say that the political scientists were reluctant to commit themselves to anything; it is they rather than the physical scientists who seemed isolated from the rest of the sample. (The extremity index for the 25 individuals affiliated with "miscellaneous" dis-

ciplines in Table 30 was 456.) Certainly the hypothesis will have
to be modified to link the social scientists to the physical scientists. In this form, the extremity index is impressive evidence
supporting the theory; however, the fact that the differences
were significant on only three of the ten specific questions made
affirmation of the hypothesis conditional.

To shift from the extremity of attitudes to their direction,
Table 37 gives responses to thirteen policy questions, which
involve major issues: attitudes toward world communism, including the threat of the Soviet Union and China, as well as that of
ideology and national power; the long-run stability of deterrence; attitudes toward American policy, including a general
analysis of the containment policy and whether the respondent
has publicly disagreed with the government in the past five years;
accountability outside of the nation-state; and the role of the
military in strategy and disarmament. It was hypothesized that
physical scientists, as opposed to political scientists, would be:
less concerned about world communism and the Soviet Union,
regarding China as the major future threat to the United States;
pessimistic about deterrence (on the basis of Levine's suggestion that attitudes on these issues are related);[14] unsympa-
thetic to the American government's policies in strategy and disarmament; in favor of widening responsibility beyond national
borders; and opposed to the military having more to say in government decisions. It was also hypothesized that social scientists
would occupy an interim position on all of these issues.

Table 37 does not support these hypotheses, although certain
predicted tendencies do appear. The differences were statistically significant on only five of the thirteen questions. Political
scientists did seem more concerned about the communist threat
in general, although they actually occupied an intermediate position between the physical and social scientists and the nonaffiliated. Physical scientists found it much easier to visualize an alli-
ance of the Soviet Union and the United States against China

14. Levine, *The Arms Debate*, pp. 44–57; see also chap. 3 above.

than the rest of the sample. On the six variables relating to communism, only three showed significant differences.

There was general agreement on the containment policy (successful) and willingness to publicly disagree with the government (high). There was less difference between the three disciplinary groups on the general threat of the Soviet Union than had been predicted; what difference that did exist suggests that social scientists were actually less concerned about Russia than the physical scientists. Although political scientists were much less impressed by the idea of world government than the rest of the sample, there was remarkably little difference on the general concept that as a nuclear superpower the United States should act as though it were responsible to the people of the world. Apparently the concept of "no annihilation without representation" had been persuasive, although political scientists were reluctant to institutionalize it. Differences on attitudes toward the military were also not as great as anticipated; the high significance figures are due to the promilitary stance of the nonaffiliated on the first indicator and the antimilitary position of the social scientists on the second.

Generally, the differences were fewer and less intense than had been expected, especially in view of the strong differences on periodicals in Table 35. Whether this unity was due to common participation in the problems involved or simply reflected a general lack of differences among members of the various disciplines is impossible to say, but it suggested that the domination of the area by a single discipline, such as political science, may not make as much of a difference as might have been expected.

the academic future of strategy and disarmament

One indication of the presence of civilians outside of government in the area of strategy and disarmament has been the development of courses dealing with the topic in college and university curriculums.[15] The importance of this should not be underestimated:

> Intellectual involvement in national security studies has spread throughout the country, producing an often overwhelming but impressive literature and, perhaps most important, providing a core of knowledgeable men who could be called into public service at the highest echelons of government. But the field's roots — and its future — must lie in the colleges and universities. For no area worthy of intellectual inquiry can be strong without good teachers.[16]

The importance of this development is increased by the fact that traditionally the military, in contrast to nearly every other profession, has had no academic counterpart; it has been suggested that this has a good deal to do with the paucity of theory in the area of strategy and disarmament.[17]

One of the basic hypotheses of this study was that there was a large reservoir of individuals who had worked in the field who would be available to teach courses on the subject in universities, especially if conventional academic requirements such as possession of the doctoral degree were relaxed. This does not seem to be true. Of the 97 respondents who had not taught a course in the field and who answered questions about whether they would *like* to do so and whether they *expected* to do so, seven both wanted to and expected to, one entrapped individual didn't want to but expected to, and only seventeen (18 percent) wanted to but didn't expect to. It is true that if all of these were brought into the area, they would make a sizable contribution, since only 31 respondents said that they had taught a course in the field before. A much larger group had been hypothesized, enabling interested schools to increase the number of such

15. P. G. Bock and Morton Berkowitz, "The Emerging Field of National Security," *World Politics* 19 (1966), p. 124, and Lyons and Morton, *Schools for Strategy*, pp. 127–99.

16. Lyons and Morton, *Schools for Strategy*, pp. 127–28.

17. Thomas C. Schelling, *The Strategy of Conflict* (Cambridge, Mass.: Harvard University Press, 1963), p. 8.

courses several times in a short time; however, there was just not that much interest in teaching such a course.

In determining the academic future of this area of study, its relationships with the established academic disciplines will be crucial, because of the structure of the university.

Within the structure of the academic world promotion and status derive from standing in an academic department and are most often the reward for work done in established fields of inquiry. In the final analysis, then, the strength of national security studies in the universities depends on acceptance by the traditional departments.[18]

There are several possibilities for the future development of the field within the universities. Question 23 asked the opinion of respondents on this subject:

Several universities are now offering courses in the field of strategy and disarmament. What do you think is the most likely academic future of this field of study?

The five alternatives and the results for the disciplinary groups and for the sample as a whole are shown in Table 38.

Based on the assertion by Lyons and Morton that political science has done more than any other discipline to include national security studies as a recognized specialty area, it was hypothesized that political scientists would see it developing as a specialty area within their own discipline, whereas the others would prefer an interdisciplinary group or a separate discipline. Table 38 confirms the hypothesis: 36 percent of the sample as a whole chose the interdisciplinary alternative, as compared with only 28 percent for a specialty field, but political scientists preferred the latter by 49 percent to 22 percent. (An implication of this hypothesis was that those who did prefer a specialty field would name political science as the discipline within which it would be placed; the data confirmed this, with 81 percent of those who

18. Lyons and Morton, *Schools for Strategy*, p. 302.

Table 38

DISCIPLINES AND ACADEMIC FUTURE OF
STRATEGY AND DISARMAMENT

Alternatives	Political Science	Physical Sciences	Other Social Sciences	Not Affiliated with an Academic Discipline	Total Sample
Development into separate discipline..................	4%	0%	7%	7%	5%
Development into recognized inter-disciplinary field such as area studies......................	22	64	53	38	36
Development into recognized specialty area within a major discipline (What discipline?).........	49	14	7	24	28
Scattered courses taught by individuals interested in area in various disciplines...............	25	22	33	29	30
No courses in area..............	0	0	0	2	1
Total	100	100	100	100	100

Note: Ns were: political science, 51; physical sciences, 14; other social sciences, 15; not affiliated with an academic discipline, 45; total sample, 145. Significance level: .05.

named a discipline choosing political science, 10 percent naming international relations, and the rest scattered; N was 41.)

The significant point about this difference is that although the sample preferred the interdisciplinary alternative, the group in the best position to influence the actual decision was the political scientists, who saw it as a specialty field within their own discipline. As shown in Table 39, 75 percent of the people who had been teaching courses in strategy and disarmament were political scientists. An even larger proportion (84 percent) of those who had not taught such a course but who expected to do so in the future were also political scientists. Although it is true that the percentage of those who would have liked to teach such a course drops to 44, the difference appears among those who were not affiliated with an academic discipline but who probably would have been willing to work within a political science department.

The general lack of support for the establishment of a new academic discipline was rather surprising, since it has been suggested before[19] and since at least one major university has seriously considered the establishment of a Ph.D. program in strategic studies. Another suggestion has been the incorporation of strategy and disarmament as a subdivision within international

19. Bock and Berkowitz, "The Emerging Field of National Security," p. 124.

Table 39

DISCIPLINES AND TEACHING IN FIELD OF STRATEGY AND DISARMAMENT

	Political Science	Physical Sciences	Other Social Sciences	Not Affiliated with an Academic Discipline	Number	Significance Level
Respondent has taught college course in strategy and disarmament (as opposed to including sections on topic within a course in related area)................	75%	4%	11%	4%	28	.001
Respondent has not taught such a course but expects to in future....	84	3	7	0	31	.001
Respondent has not taught such a course but would like to in future.........................	44	7	7	33	45	.001

relations;[20] in fact, of those who wanted it within a discipline, 10 percent named international relations, making it the only candidate other than political science to be named by more than one individual. However, the data suggest that international relations instead provides a model of the progression of a problem area from insignificance to an interdisciplinary area to a specialty area within a discipline. As far as our sample is concerned, international relations is now a specialty field of political science; of the 19 respondents who took their highest degree in this field, as opposed to political science, 15 said they regarded themselves as affiliated with political science, one each named law and operations research, one was not affiliated with a discipline, and one did not know whether he was or not.

It is important to keep in mind that the decisions about the academic future of the field are not going to be made by taking a poll of individuals working in it; they will be made by university administrators, who will be influenced almost exclusively by the individuals who are teaching courses in the area. Given the data on the dominance of political scientists among those who have taught such courses and who expect to do so in the future, it seems likely that the study of strategy and disarmament will make the shift from an interdisciplinary field to a specialty area of political science considerably more quickly than did international relations.

20. Ibid.; and J. W. Burton, " 'Peace Research' and 'International Relations,' " *Journal of Conflict Resolution* 8 (1964), 281–86.

chapter seven

professionalism in
strategy and disarmament

As Wesley Posvar suggests, the private nuclear strategists are an occupational skill group.

Strategy expertise is the product of men, organizations, and methods.
It would be insufficient, however, to represent these men simply as
actors in a system or a class society. For the strategy experts do make
up a community. It is a community with a degree of coherence that
seems to exceed the bonds of common organization and shared technique.

So the question of the nature of the strategy community has a special significance. We are obliged to apply the tests of professionalism
and elitism in order to adequately comprehend the community.[1]

In examining the development of the study of strategy and
disarmament, the concept of the profession provides an obvious
and useful entrance, although it will be suggested that it not be

1. Posvar, "Strategy Expertise and National Security," p. 49.

overworked. It is obvious because of the professional status of its chief competitor, the military;[2] this, in turn, stems from the problem of responsibility of a group of men who manage the sole legitimate source of armed power within a state, and this problem of responsibility remains for the private nuclear strategist, although in somewhat different form. The concept of profession is valuable because it suggests several interesting areas of investigation.

There is a good deal of literature, sociological and otherwise, on the subject of professions and professionalism.[3] Most of it is based on the assumption that the term is a concept that can be defined and against which various skill groups can be compared to see if they should be classified as professions or not. Howard Becker, however, has persuasively suggested that, as used in our society, it refers to a morally desirable kind of work and that the criteria discussed at such length are rather ineffective attempts to construct an intellectual framework for this moral judgment.

We can instead take a radically sociological view, regarding professions simply as those occupations which have been fortunate enough in the politics of today's work world to gain and maintain possession of that honorific title. On this view, there is no such thing as the "true" profession and no set of characteristics necessarily associated with the title. There are only those work groups which are commonly regarded as professions and those which are not.

Such a definition takes as central the fact that "profession" is an honorific title, a term of approbation. It recognizes that "profession" is a collective symbol and one that is highly valued.[4]

2. This status is in fact a relatively recent development; much of the early literature treats the military as either a bureaucracy or a remnant of the feudal and aristocratic tradition (Huntington, *Soldier and the State*, pp. 7–18, 469).

3. For excellent bibliographies, see Huntington, *Soldier and the State*, pp. 469–70, and the notes in Howard S. Becker, "The Nature of a Profession," in Nelson B. Henry (ed.), *Education for the Professions*, Sixty-first Yearbook of the National Society for the Study of Education, Part II (Chicago: University of Chicago Press, 1962), pp. 27–46.

4. Becker, "The Nature of a Profession," pp. 32–33.

This suggests the limitations of the concept. Since most of the literature on the subject is concerned with establishing such characteristics and whether a given occupation has them, this viewpoint suggests that it is irrelevant, at least in determining whether a particular vocation is a profession. The qualification is important; whereas the corporate nature of medicine, for instance, may not determine whether it is a profession, it is certainly an important characteristic of the field. Similarly we shall be concerned with certain concepts usually related to professionalism for their own sake rather than to determine whether the study of strategy and disarmament is developing into a new profession.

The symbol *profession* is a valuable one; by implying the moral value of the work being done, it legitimatizes a skill group. Therefore, it is perhaps not surprising that most of the sample asserted that the study of strategy and disarmament is developing into a new profession; specifically, 68 percent of the sample agreed with this statement (Question 45), and only 25 percent disagreed (N was 158). Interestingly enough, younger respondents were more likely to agree; 64 percent of those born between 1900 and 1919 agreed, as compared with 76 percent of those born between 1920 and 1939, and the significance level of the difference was .01.

The symbol *profession* involves several different concepts; though different authors may interpret it in various ways, the differences tend to be in the extra features added rather than in the basic structure. It assumes the existence of an intellectual expertise that requires extensive preparation to master. This expertise, moreover, is important to society. Because of the long period of preparation involved, members of a profession have a monopoly on this expertise. Because of this monopoly, members of a profession can only be judged by other members; outsiders do not possess the requisite knowledge. Because of this responsibility, a profession incorporates a professional ethic, a responsibility to society as a whole or to the client who pays for the services of the professional. Thus there are two qualities stressed extensively in the literature: *corporateness* and *responsibility*. A third, which is usually assumed but not often mentioned, is that a profession is a *full-time activity*.[5] We will examine the study of strategy and disarmament in terms of each of these ideas.

full time versus part time

Other observers have noted the prevalence of individuals working in strategy and disarmament on a part-time basis.[6] At the outset of the study it was obvious that this would be true of at least part of our population. There were 500 individuals in the population, a figure larger than any of the estimates of full-time personnel in the field. A typical tabulation is that of Wesley Posvar:

The most highly organized strategy expertise is concentrated in half a dozen research corporations. . . . Of their combined professional staffs numbering less than two thousand, perhaps only a hundred can be regarded as specialists in strategy at the national policy level; the remainder are scientists and technologists who work on elements of our defense posture without primary regard for the whole.[7]

Questions 11, 12, and 13 were concerned with this problem; the results are shown in Table 40. The data confirm the hypothesis that over half of the sample would spend less than half of their professional time in the area. The table also suggests two trends: general stability (half of the group had not significantly altered the portion of their time in the field in the past five years, and three-quarters did not expect it to change in the next five) with a small tendency for the percentage of those decreasing their activity to be larger than the percentage increasing. The latter could be offset by a rather small number of individuals entering the field.

5. See footnote 3 above.
6. Archibald, "Social Science Approaches to Peace," pp. 99–100.
7. Posvar, "Strategy Expertise and National Security," p. 58.

Table 40

PERCENTAGE OF PROFESSIONAL TIME SPENT IN
FIELD OF STRATEGY AND DISARMAMENT

Question	Response
About what percentage of your professional time do you currently spend in work related to strategy and disarmament?	
0-25	57%
26-50	13
51-75	12
76-100	18
Total	100

(N=187)

Question	Response
In the past five years, has this percentage	
substantially increased?	22%
not substantially changed?	49
substantially decreased?	29
Total	100

(N=175)

Question	Response
Five years from now, do you expect this percentage to have	
substantially increased?	9%
not substantially changed?	75
substantially decreased?	16
Total	100

(N=134)

It was hypothesized that those individuals who were currently spending over half of their professional time in the field would be higher on indicators of status and influence than on the rest of the sample. Table 41 suggests that, although there is some support for this hypothesis, the influence of those working only part time in the area should not be underestimated. On all the eleven indicators part-time people composed over half of the more influential group. Their influence was especially clear in the area of full-time employment by various institutions; only in the case of private research institutes was the difference between

Table 41

PORTION OF PROFESSIONAL TIME SPENT IN STRATEGY AND
DISARMAMENT AND INDICATORS OF STATUS AND INFLUENCE

Status and Influence Indicators	51-100%	0-50%	Number	Significance Level*
Sample.......................................	30	70	187	
Perceived Influentials.........................	43	57	40	.10
Publication Point Scores over 15................	48	52	25	.01
Worked on Government Research Contract in Strategy and Disarmament...................	39	61	88	.05
Full-time Employment in Strategy and Disarmament, by Type of Institution:				
College (teaching)........................	36	64	44	NS
College (non-teaching)....................	47	53	19	.15
College research institute.................	36	64	28	NS
Private research institute..................	49	51	63	.001
Private Corporation.......................	44	56	16	NS
Periodical...............................	29	71	17	NS
Federal government.......................	31	69	36	NS
Other institutions.........................	29	71	7	NS

* Based on chi square statistic.

the two groups significant above the .05 level. This in turn suggests that this is the only type of institution that really specializes in the study of strategy and disarmament; for the others such work tends to be somewhat intermittent. This might change at universities if the field seemed likely to develop into a separate discipline; however, its likely development into a specialty area within political science[8] will probably continue the status quo, with teachers giving courses in other areas as well.

Mentioned in the discussion of academic disciplines was the general hypothesis that those who saw their work in strategy and disarmament as closely related to their profession would be influ-

8. See pp. 112–17.

enced more by intellectual than by policy motives than would those whose work in the field was not related to their profession. This, in turn, generated the hypothesis that political scientists would be more influenced by intellectual motives, physical and social scientists by policy motives; Table 34 confirmed this hypothesis.[9] Using the same hypothesis, it was expected that those spending more than half of their professional time in the field would be more influenced by intellectual motives, and the others would be more concerned with policy motives. The hypothesis could not be substantiated; although seven of the nine motives did vary in the expected direction, none of the differences was significant.

Generally, the differences between those spending more than half and those spending less than half of their professional time within the area were less than had been expected. Certainly there was no basis for concluding that the part-timers were discriminated against or that there was any serious split between the two groups.

corporateness

The tendency toward corporateness in a profession is a natural consequence of the fact that its members possess a monopoly on a socially important expertise; therefore, a member's performance can only be judged by other members, since other individuals lack the necessary knowledge. It is worth noting that this, like the other characteristics we shall examine, is an ideal that has not been reached by any of the professions; even in medicine, which has stressed this idea, the patient is able to change doctors because of dissatisfaction, and there is evidence that this possibility affects the professional actions of physicians.[10]

9. See p. 103.

10. Eliot Freidson, "Client Control and Medical Practice," *American Journal of Sociology* 65 (1960), 374–82, cited in Becker, "The Nature of a Profession," p. 44.

Nevertheless, the concept is important as a symbol, and in many cases it is the major reason for seeking the title of a profession for a given skill group.

Most important, professional status is a solution to one of the chronic problems of work groups which regularly deal with a lay public, the problem of the layman who feels that he knows more about the work being done than the man who has devoted his life to it. When a group is able to convince the public that it is a profession, one of the rewards is a public readiness to abdicate the right to criticize. . . . *This confines criticism and possible interference or punishment within the group of like-minded professionals, people who operate with a fundamentally similar view of the problems of their kind of work and of the appropriate kinds of solutions to them.* . . . Because most work groups feel that they know more about their work than those with whom they deal, the status of professional is greatly desired and eagerly sought.[11]

The implication that corporateness may limit the range of thought and ideas suggests that its development may not be desirable. It is worth keeping in mind, when discussing the question of professionalism, that civilians are involved deeply in strategy and disarmament precisely because another profession, the military, was unable to meet the new challenges in its prescribed field of expertise. If protection from uninformed lay criticism is one side of the coin of corporateness in strategy and disarmament, the other is Talleyrand's observation that war is too important to be left to the generals. Rather surprisingly, our sample apparently had no difficulty in resolving the problem. Question 58, which was answered on a seven-point agree-disagree scale, stated:

The issues of strategy and disarmament are so complex that it is impossible to conduct meaningful public discussion about them; they are best left to the experts and specialists, under the general guidance of political leaders.

11. Howard S. Becker, "Some Problems of Professionalization," *Adult Education* 6 (1956), p. 102 (emphasis added).

Table 42

PRESUMED CONSEQUENCES OF PUBLISHING MATERIAL
DISAPPROVED OF BY "ESTABLISHMENT"

Probable Result	Agree	Perhaps
Not listened to by government......................	33%	7%
Difficulty in obtaining research funds.................	15	9
Loss of general respect among colleagues............	13	8
Difficulty in obtaining good university appointments.....	8	10
No effect; there is no "establishment".................	17	10
No effect; the "establishment" has no real power........	14	9
Other:		
The "establishment" exists, but judges work on its merits.......................................	10	4
The "establishment" exists, but has no real power over respondent................................	9	1
Difficulty in getting published......................	7	2
Respondent has already had trouble with the "establishment".................................	3	5
There is more than one "establishment"..............	3	2
Other answers implying existence of "establishment...	21	5

Note: Total responding, 144.

A full 90 percent disagreed with this statement, and only 9 percent agreed (*N* was 177). Our respondents were not interested
in limiting public debate, presumably even at the cost of a certain amount of uninformed criticism. Whatever the motives
behind their perception of the field as a new profession, exclusion from public criticism did not seem to be one of them.

Most of the established professions display their corporateness
by their control of the recruitment and admission of new members. At its extreme this control may be supported by the state,

as in the cases of medicine, law, and the military. Another manifestation may be the power of the professions to expel a member and, by so doing, to prevent him from practicing; again this power may be enforced by the state. It is clear that the institutions to do these things simply do not exist in the field of strategy and disarmament, and it is unlikely that there would be much support for their development. However, this does not dispose of the question; more subtle influences may well be at work. To probe into this area, Question 37 asked:

It has been suggested that there is an "establishment" in the field of strategy and disarmament, a group which sets the limits (perhaps unconsciously) within which strategic debate and discussion is carried on. If you published material of which the "establishment" disapproved, what effects do you think this would have on you? (Check as many as you feel are appropriate.)

Table 42 shows the results of this question. Aside from the six alternatives listed on the questionnaire, the five mentioned most frequently as "other" were also coded. There was general agreement that an "establishment" exists; 117 respondents (81 percent) checked at least one consequence. However, there was no agreement on the consequences to the individual if he were to take actions of which the group would not approve; the perception of the "establishment" was hazy at best. None of the alternatives received the support of half of the sample; the most frequently named was "not listened to by the government," with 33 percent agreeing and another 7 percent uncertain.

Generally there was little difference within the sample on these questions. One partial exception concerns those individuals who had worked on government research contracts in strategy and disarmament, as shown in Table 43. Although there were significant and interesting differences between these two groups, the first thing to note is that they were relatively small; they were significant at the .05 level on only four of the twelve alternatives, and neither group mustered half of its membership behind any single consequence.

On the other hand, those who had worked on government research contracts were clearly less concerned about the existence and effects of the "establishment," at least in terms of external sanctions. Thus they were less concerned that they might lose

Table 43

PRESUMED CONSEQUENCES OF OPPOSING "ESTABLISHMENT" AND
EXPERIENCE ON GOVERNMENT RESEARCH CONTRACTS*

Probable Result	Yes	No	Significance Level
Not listened to by government..............	28%	38%	.05
Difficulty in obtaining research funds.......	16	15	.10
Loss of general respect among colleagues............................	20	7	.01
Difficulty in obtaining good university appointments..........................	9	8	NS
No effect; there is no "establishment".......	22	14	.10
No effect; the "establishment" has no real power................................	9	19	.15
Other: The "establishment" exists, but judges work on its merits....................	17	1	.001
The "establishment" exists, but has no power over respondent...............	3	15	.05
Difficulty in getting published............	6	8	NS
Respondent has already had trouble with the "establishment....................	5	3	NS
There is more than one "establishment"....	6	0	.10
Other answers implying existence of "establishment"......................	22	21	NS
(Number)	(64)	(73)	

* Respondents answering "Yes" to question "Have you ever worked on a government research contract in the area of nuclear strategy and disarmament?"

their governmental audience, had more confidence in the basis of the judgments of the "establishment," and were somewhat more skeptical of its existence.

We have noted previously that corporateness involves sanctions by members of the profession against other members. Thus it is interesting that those who had worked on government contracts were more concerned about the loss of respect of their colleagues than were those who had not done such work; although such disapproval is hardly comparable to disbarment, it remains a significant sanction that may be exercised and a useful indicator of corporateness. It is worth noting that, of the twelve alternatives, ten are specific consequences of the existence of the "establishment." (This excludes "the 'establishment' does not exist" and "others.") Respondents who had worked on government research contracts ranked loss of respect among colleagues second only to possible loss of an audience in the government, whereas for those who had not done such work it was ranked seventh among ten. On the other hand, its importance should not be exaggerated; only 20 percent of those who had worked on government research contracts checked it.

Generally, corporateness is less highly developed among those working in strategy and disarmament than might have been expected. There was a general unwillingness to remove the subject from public discussion into the realm of "experts"; and though there was a general apprehension of the existence of some sort of "establishment," there was no agreement on the sanctions it might command.

It is worth asking why this is true. One reason is probably that the difficulties in dealing with the public are less than in some other skill groups who desire the status of profession in order to gain some autonomy—education and social work, for example. These groups work with the public at large, truly the lay public, whereas under normal circumstances only a small part of the public is interested in questions of strategy and disarmament—

even less than is interested in foreign policy.[12] The public that is interested in these affairs tends to be better educated and thus probably less likely to ask completely uninformed questions. Moreover, the study of strategy and disarmament has the advantage of being related to a recognized profession, the military; it seems to receive from this status some degree of immunity from casual public criticism. It is remarkable how many intelligent people have no knowledge of even the basic concepts of strategy and disarmament and who feel inhibited from criticising by the allegedly "technical" nature of the issues involved.

A third reason is probably a lack of confidence in their own expertise. It is difficult to document this lack of confidence; there were no questions designed to probe attitudes on the "state of the art." However, comments on various questions and observations in interviews, as well as published statements, suggest that it does exist. One respondent, for instance, when asked who he thought had done the most significant work in the field, listed some names and then added, "No one has really done much." The first chapter of Thomas C. Schelling's landmark book *The Strategy of Conflict* is called "The Retarded Science of International Strategy"; in it he observes:

What is impressive is not how complicated the idea of deterrence has become, and how carefully it has been refined and developed, but how slow the process has been, how vague the concepts still are, and how inelegant the current theory of deterrence is. . . . There is no scientific literature on deterrence that begins to compare with, say, the literature on inflation, Asiatic flue, elementary-school reading or smog.[13]

12. Bernard C. Cohen, "The Military Policy Public," *Public Opinion Quarterly* 30 (1966), 200–211.
13. P. 7. Further evidence of this attitude may be found in the author's "Simulation and the Private Nuclear Strategists," Simulated International Processes, Department of Political Science, Northwestern University, 1967.

A fourth possible reason is the general lack of coherence of the strategic community. We have noted the variety of institutions that employ individuals working full time in the field;[14] other authors have noted the wide variety of views on policy among them.[15] Wesley Posvar has suggested that this pragmatic, pluralistic system reflects the American dislike for big government and militarism.[16] Given this system, and the accompanying problems of communication, the role of periodicals other than professional journals in connecting this disparate group should not be overlooked.[17] If participation in the strategic debate is limited to the "experts," the problem of deciding who is an "expert" must be considered. This situation is not unique in strategy and disarmament.

With a new profession the first generation cannot have a complete formal training in the principles and techniques of the profession, for these are still in the process of being discovered. Nor can they have the "proper academic qualifications," for these are still to be decided on. And so the founders are a little less than perfect, perhaps even a source of slight embarrassment to the succeeding generations of professionals they train. The great sociologists of the last century (and some of the great in this century) did not have degrees in sociology, although they granted them, and many great educators never studied in a school of education, though they may have taught in one. This kind of situation leads to difficulties when the effort to enforce professional standards of training and competence is strong, for those who are to be ruled out by these standards may point (perhaps with some justice) to the example of the founding fathers.[18]

There is no evidence that this situation will soon change. Soci-

---

14. See chap. 5.

15. Levine, *The Arms Debate*; Herzog, *The War-Peace Establishment*.

16. "Strategy Expertise and National Security," p. 3.

17. An analogy is the role of the press in foreign affairs, informing officials what other branches of their own government are doing; see Bernard C. Cohen, *The Press and Foreign Policy* (Princeton, N.J.: Princeton University Press, 1963), pp. 208–47.

18. Becker, "Some Problems of Professionalization," p. 104.

ology and education instituted academic programs; when the older generation died out, academic standards of admission could be applied. There is no evidence that such programs will be developed in strategy and disarmament or that the borders of the strategic community will be more clearly defined in the foreseeable future. The problem is further complicated by the existence of many individuals working only part time in the area, as suggested in the previous section. All in all, the general openness of the field seems likely to continue into the future; considering the magnitude of the problems and the paucity of the tools, this is probably just as well.

responsibility

Posvar has observed:

For all his attention to practical things like hardware and money, despite his concern (hopefully) with philosophical abstractions like power, the strategist must be affected by the fact that he dwells in the macrocosm. His reach is intercontinental, his resources are scaled in national wealth, his memory encompasses all of recorded history, his aspirations exist in the form of ideology, and the stakes of his actions are the survival and well-being of societies. However far fetched or impudent this analogy may seem, there can be no question that these are the terms in which the strategist must think, at least part of the time, and this is the scale of the consequences of the actions which he helps determine.[19]

The service that a profession performs is of such importance to society that its members must have an ethic of responsibility; the monopoly of this expertise is granted on the condition that it not be used solely, or even primarily, for the profit of the practitioners.[20] This is notably true of the military profession. Samuel Huntington states the classic professional military ethic:

19. "Strategy Expertise and National Security," p. 193.
20. See above, note 3.

The expertise of the officer imposes upon him a special social responsibility. The employment of his expertise promiscuously for his own advantage would wreck the fabric of society. . . . While all professions are to some extent regulated by the state, the military profession is monopolized by the state. . . . While the primary responsibility of the physician is to his patient, and the lawyer to his client, the principal responsibility of the military officer is to the state.[21]

Two events in World War II brought this rather simple view into serious question. The first, and less well-known, was the dilemma of the French army after its defeat in 1940. Its traditional loyalty to the state dictated acceptance of the Vichy government and cooperation with the Germans against the Allies. However, the existence of the Free French forces under the command of Charles de Gaulle gave the French officers the alternative to fight on against Germany, even at the cost of revolting against the state. The end of World War II and the victory of the Allies *legitimized* this revolt against the state; this experience, in part, explains the army's similar actions after later defeats in Indo-China and Algeria.[22] The second experience, of course, was the participation of the German army in both the planning of aggressive war and the genocide policies of the Third Reich; these issues reached a climax at the Nuremberg trials and set off a debate on the professional ethics of the soldier that has not yet been resolved.[23] Briefly, the French army had diffi-

21. *Soldier and the State*, pp. 14–16.

22. For a penetrating study of this event, see Paul-Marie de la Gorce, *The French Army: A Military-Political History* (New York: George Braziller, 1963), pp. 308–37.

23. For contrasting views of the experience of the German Army, see Walter Goerlitz, *History of the German General Staff, 1657–1945* (New York: Frederick A. Praeger, Inc., 1953), pp. 204–499; and Gordon A. Craig, *The Politics of the Prussian Army, 1640–1945* (New York: Oxford University Press, 1964), pp. 427–503. For contrasting views of the Nuremberg trials and the German Army, see Eugene Davidson, *The Trial of the Germans: Nuremberg, 1945–1946* (New York: Macmillan Company, 1966), pp. 31–426; and Victor H. Bernstein, *Final Judgment: The Story of Nuremberg* (New York: Boni & Gaer, 1947). An interesting commentary on the

culty determining the identity of the state and its interests; the German army found that it was supposed to have a loyalty even above that to the state—to some concepts of humanity in general.

Although the nature of the officer's code may be in doubt, the reasons for its existence are not. The justification for such a code is obvious; the professional military is the sole legitimate instrument of mass violence and, as such, the ultimate element of political power. The problem of insuring its responsibility to the state is obvious; without such responsibility it could simply take over the state and set up its own government.

It has been suggested that civilians working in strategy and disarmament do not have such an ethic.[24] Indeed, the need for it is less obvious. Civilians outside of government, after all, have no direct control over the instruments of military power; by themselves they are unable to overthrow a government, although they might be important participants in such a conspiracy. Generally, they serve government only as advisers, and their influence may be even more indirect when exercised through public writings and discussion. Nevertheless, the quotation at the beginning of this section reminds us of the magnitude of the issues with which they work. Given their considerable influence in decisions in nuclear strategy and disarmament, a case can be made that they should act on the basis of the interests of society at large rather than their own particular interests or those of particular governmental institutions. Posvar suggests one formulation, essentially a broadening of the professional military ethic:

While responsibility in the form of accountability may be measured and allocated to individuals in proportion to the power which they exercise, the need to commit oneself to the interest of the state is not parcelled out among strategists in relation to their institutional re-

---

implications of nuclear weapons in this area is Guenter Levy, "Superior Orders, Nuclear Warfare, and the Dictates of Conscience: The Dilemma of Military Obedience in the Atomic Age," *American Political Science Review* 55 (1961), 1–23.

24. Posvar, "Strategy Expertise and National. Security," p. 53.

moteness from the strings of power. This shared responsibility is an indivisable entity, and, like hydraulic pressure, it exerts the same force on all points of the surface which it covers. It falls fully upon all who serve as strategists. It rests equally, and heavily, upon the President, the Secretary of Defense, the RAND analyst, the Pentagon staff officer, and the professor — whoever gives counsel or exercises choice regarding the security of the United States. It is an ubiquitous sword of Damocles bringing discomfort to everyone who contributes to strategic decisions. Max Weber said, "Whoever contracts with violent means for whatever ends — and every politician does — is exposed to its specific consequences. . . . He lets himself in for the diabolic forces lurking in all violence." This is the unavoidable, morbid, and shared burden of those who make strategy.[25]

Although this is a useful starting point, it has at least two obvious difficulties. The first is the single-minded dedication to the interest of the state. Aside from ignoring the implications of the Nuremberg verdicts, this rests on the implicit assumption that the nation-state will remain the ultimate political unit. This is probably true, but a case can be made that the development of nuclear weapons has made the nation-state obsolete, at least in terms of providing security for its citizens.[26] If this argument is accepted, it suggests that individuals, presumably including those working in nuclear strategy and disarmament, should work for the development of international institutions for the control of such weapons—possibly a world government as such. Such an imperative would force the individual to subordinate the interests of his nation-state to the needs of some form of world order.

If accepted, this responsibility falls with special force upon the strategic community. The area of nuclear arms control is perhaps

25. Ibid., p. 266; the quotation is from Max Weber, *From Max Weber: Essays in Sociology*, translated and edited by H. H. Gerth and C. Wright Mills (New York: Oxford University Press, 1958), pp. 124–25.

26. John Herz, *International Politics in the Atomic Age* (New York: Columbia University Press, 1959), pp. 96–108; but compare his "The Territorial State Revisited: Reflections on the Future of the Nation-State," *Polity* 1 (1968), 12–34.

the only major issue on which the United States and the Soviet Union have both stated repeatedly that cooperation is essential. If we are indeed to proceed beyond the nation-state, the field of nuclear weapons policy is the most likely field where progress will begin. Moreover, within the strategic community, the private nuclear strategists will have the heaviest initial responsibility. Working outside of the constraints of present government policy, they are the group most competent to establish the theories and conceptual framework from which political change may come. The problems are not entirely dissimilar to those of the French and German officers in World War II. Is "the interest of the state" the continued existence of most of its population or of its government, if the choice is reduced to these? May an individual give precedence to "the interest of the state" over all considerations of humanity; if not, what are these considerations?

The second limitation of this formulation is its generality. It is the kind of statement that most individuals could accept, but it is dubious that it would mean much in practice. There are few activities that cannot be subsumed under the rubric of "national interest" (or "international interest," for that matter). In order to probe this problem in a mail questionnaire, it was necessary to narrow the subject considerably. That the influence of civilians outside of government on government decisions is necessarily indirect complicates the question. It was decided to focus on the problem of government research contracts because in this case the influence is somewhat more direct and deliberate than in open publication. Question 61, which was answered on a seven-point agree-disagree scale, stated:

A researcher has a moral responsibility for the consequences of his work in government policy decisions.

Any reference to the question of whether the consequences were logically foreseeable by the researcher was deliberately omitted in an attempt to elicit response from a moral rather than a legal standpoint. Of the sample, 83 percent agreed with the statement, and only 12 percent disagreed (*N* was 171; it excluded both those who said "Don't know" and those who gave responses but changed the question by inserting qualifications). Generally there was agreement among the sample on the question; one

Table 44

**GOVERNMENT CONTRACTS ON WHICH RESPONDENTS
WOULD REFUSE TO WORK FOR MORAL OR POLITICAL REASONS**

Type of Contract	Yes*	Perhaps*
Techniques for staging military coup in U.S.	67%	3%
Establishment of Doomsday Machine by U.S.	64	6
Strategy for combating revolution in U.S. with nuclear weapons	56	4
Technique for starting catalytic war between Soviet Union and China	56	2
Techniques and utility of preventive war launched by U.S.	46	4
Techniques and violating existing arms control agreement by U.S.	46	7
Techniques for violating prospective agreement on complete and general disarmament by U.S.	41	6
Unilateral disarmament by U.S.	34	5
No government contract would be refused for political or moral reasons	11	3
Establishment of world government	8	2
Other:		
Other similar examples	10	4
Other responses suggesting that, though the question is badly phrased and does not get at real issues, there are moral considerations to be taken into consideration	10	4

Note: Total responding, 169.

* "Yes" indicates percentage of respondents who said they would refuse to work on such a contract; "perhaps," those who said they would work on it under certain specified conditions.

notable exception was that only 67 percent of the ex-military group (defined as having reached the rank of captain or lieutenant commander or higher) agreed, whereas 87 percent of the rest of the sample did (Ns were 36 and 133 respectively; the differences were significant at the .001 level). This difference was not unexpected, given the military tradition of obedience to superior orders and the consequent upward transfer of responsibility. However, that such a large percentage of the sample agreed with the statement suggested that the question was a legitimate one in the view of the respondents and that further investigation into the matter might be useful.

This further investigation involved the most controversial question of the study, judging from comments on the questionnaire. Question 41 read:

Can you imagine any government contract on which you would refuse to work for political or moral reasons? Please check any of the following on which you would refuse to work.

It was not the question itself that aroused such concern but the alternatives listed; they are given in Table 44, along with the percentage of respondents checking each. Because of the reaction to this question, a brief explanation of it is in order. Given an interest in the moral aspect of government research contracts, their subjects were an obvious way to discriminate between those that would and would not be accepted. Specific examples were included because they made the question more specific and meant that the sample was responding to the same thing. Without examples, it seemed likely that some people would simply review the last few contract proposals they had heard about to answer the question, and others would dream up even more startling possibilities than these; thus the answers of these two groups would not really be comparable, but there would be no way to tell that from the questionnaire results.

Most of the comment, however, has centered on the hypothetical contracts. They were deliberately extreme, in order to bring out any underlying system of values that might not be invoked by "normal" contract proposals. However, it should be stressed that the author felt, then and now, that none of the nine specific suggestions was an inconceivable subject for an actual government contract. This certainly does not mean that any were considered likely, but none is impossible. The most unlikely is probably the study of techniques for staging a military coup; should the eventuality ever arise, it is unlikely that it would be studied by a formal research contract, although civilians felt to be sympathetic might be consulted informally. On the other hand, a government concerned about the possibility might want to study how it could be done; this is the kind of problem involved in doing such work. Should it be studied in order to make it more unlikely, or should it be ignored since study would make such knowledge available to those who might be tempted to put it to use, thus bringing about the event that the contract was designed to help prevent? The problem is especially acute here since such a study might well reveal that a coup could be carried out fairly easily, although just what would be done afterward might be quite a problem.

However, this possibility was included primarily because it is the fundamental question of civil-military relations, and it seemed important to see how the sample would react to it. A second question on possible domestic use of force was included, this time in support of the government in power: use of nuclear weapons against a revolution in the United States. The current racial problems might conceivably lead to the consideration of this possibility.

The Doomsday Machine question was included because it is the classic example of pushing a sound theory to a self-defeating extreme; this was precisely the reason that Herman Kahn developed the concept.[27] The question of the United States launching a preventive war was actually a serious topic of discussion and

27. Herman Kahn, *On Thermonuclear War* (Princeton, N.J.: Princeton University Press, 1961), pp. 144-53.

debate several years ago.[28] The continued technological race means that a future American government might be faced with a choice between eventual surrender and preventive war; equally important, it might *think* it was faced with this choice. Catalytic war might be an alternative to preventive war in this situation, as well as others such as an impending Sino-Soviet nuclear attack on Japan or a Russian move into Western Europe—in Kahn's terms, a failure of Type II deterrence.

Of the nine hypothetical contract proposals, two were designed to be "left wing": unilateral disarmament and world government. The other two alternatives were paired: techniques for violating an existing arms control agreement and a proposed disarmament agreement. The hypothesis was that studying the latter would be more legitimate, since it could well be examined to insure that it could not be violated if put into effect, whereas the former would seem more likely to lead to actual violation. To further increase the difference, the proposed agreement was specified as complete and general disarmament, whereas the existing one was only for arms control. The implication (admittedly not necessarily valid) was that the proposed agreement would have more important effects on the United States, especially if it could be violated successfully; studying it would therefore be more necessary.

This question was also criticized on the ground that it made respondents appear to support some rather appalling policies simply because they were willing to study them. The intent of the question was quite otherwise. There is an excellent and persuasive case to be made that any of these horrible possibilities should be studied in order to make their actual occurrence less likely.[29] The complexities of the decision have been suggested in the brief discussion of the military coup and the arms control

28. For a summary of the relevant arguments, see Bernard Brodie, *Strategy in the Missile Age* (Princeton, N.J.: Princeton University Press, 1959), pp. 226–32.
29. The classic statement is Herman Kahn's "In Defense of Thinking," which is reprinted as the first chapter of his *Thinking about the Unthinkable* (New York: Horizon Press, 1962), pp. 17–37.

and disarmament agreements. The possibility that Table 44 would be misinterpreted against the specific statement by the author did not seem to justify its omission; if it is permissible to think about these questions, surely it is legitimate to consider not thinking about them. Moreover, those who objected to the question as inappropriate had their responses coded appropriately; the 10 percent who did so, combined with the 11 percent who would not refuse any government contract for moral or political reasons, do not compose a majority of our sample.

None of this is to deny the limitations of this rather crude indicator in the analysis of a very important, complex, and emotional area of interest. An attempt to reduce the moral positions taken by many people to a single comparable measure inevitably involves some distortion; the reader may judge for himself whether this distortion is so great as to invalidate the conclusions drawn from the results.

Table 44 suggests that there was indeed some sort of ethic among our sample in its choice of government contracts. The idea of studying means of applying their expertise domestically was not well received; the military coup and nuclear suppression of a domestic revolution were first and third on the list of nine hypothetical contracts. There was also a good deal of distaste for the Doomsday Machine, catalytic war, and preventive war contracts (numbers two, four, and five respectively).

Interestingly enough, the expected difference between studying techniques for violating an existing arms control agreement and a proposed agreement for general and complete disarmament did not materialize. It was not expected that 41 percent of the sample would refuse to work on ways to violate a proposed disarmament agreement; there was more unwillingness to do this than to study unilateral disarmament. Indeed, it was striking that the two alternatives rejected least often were unilateral disarmament and world government. World government is a rather respectable policy position in some circles; however, that only 34 percent would not study unilateral disarmament was a surprise, since this is not a policy position often advocated in public.

This is perhaps a good place to reaffirm the statement that willingness to work on a contract on one of these subjects does not imply support for it as a policy. We have seen that only 8 percent of the sample said that they would refuse to work on a contract studying ways to establish world government. However, 29 percent disagreed with the statement, Question 56:

Some form of world government is the only long-term solution to the problem of the destructiveness of modern weapons and opposing nationalisms.

We shall study two divisions within the sample on the questions —ex-military versus others—to compare individuals who have worked within the ethical system of the American military with those who have and have not worked on a government research contract, because they are the individuals who have had to make such decisions in the past and are more likely to do so in the future. Table 45 shows the percentage of ex-military respondents and the rest of the sample who would refuse to work on the hypothetical contracts for political or moral reasons.

It was hypothesized that the ex-military respondents would be more willing to work on any government research contract, and, indeed, a larger percentage said that they would not refuse any government contract for moral or political reasons. However, even among the ex-military only 17 percent selected this option. Moreover, of the nine hypothetical contracts, the ex-military group was *less* willing to study unilateral disarmament and world government; the differences were statistically significant at the .08 and .05 levels respectively. This suggests that the ex-military group had a different ethical standard than the rest of the sample.

On the other hand, both groups were least reluctant to study the establishment of world government; the difference in the *ranking* of unilateral disarmament was stronger (fifth by the ex-military, eighth by the others), and catalytic war was ranked eighth by the ex-military and third by the others. The finding that the ex-military opposed unilateral disarmament more than

Table 45

EX-MILITARY* AND REFUSAL OF CONTRACTS
FOR MORAL OR POLITICAL REASONS

	Ex-Military	Others	Significance Level
Techniques for staging a military coup in U. S.	51%	71%	.08
Establishment of Doomsday Machine by U.S.	51	68	.20
Strategy for combatting revolution in U.S. with nuclear weapons	54	57	NS
Technique for starting catalytic war between Soviet Union and China	26	65	.001
Techniques and utility of preventive war launched by U.S.	31	50	.15
Techniques for violating existing arms control agreement by U.S.	46	46	NS
Techniques for violating prospective agreement on complete and general disarmament by U.S.	37	43	NS
Unilateral disarmament by U.S.	46	30	.08
No government contract would be refused for political or moral reasons	17	10	NS
Establishment of world government	17	5	.05
Other: Other similar examples	6	11	NS
Other responses suggesting that, though the question is badly phrased and does not get at real issues, there are moral considerations to be taken into consideration	14	8	.08
(Number)	(35)	(131)	

* "Ex-military" refers to those individuals who had attained the rank of captain (army or air force) or lieutenant commander (navy) or higher.

the rest of the sample was not too surprising, especially since the sample as a whole had a rather low reluctance to study the question. It is less clear that the very large difference in the two groups in their willingness to study techniques to start a catalytic war between the Soviet Union and China is significant, especially since there was less difference on willingness to study techniques of preventive war. That only two of the nine alternatives were ranked drastically differently by the two groups suggests that the differences between the groups are not as great as had been expected. It is also interesting that the ex-military perceived a greater difference between studying techniques for violating existing and proposed agreements than did the rest of the sample.

In his study of the professional military, Morris Janowitz suggested that religion might be related to the military role. He found that military leaders tended to be of the traditional Protestant denominations, especially Episcopal, although there was evidence that Catholics were coming into the officer corps in significant numbers.

Is there any special significance in the concentration of Episcopalians among the military elite, a concentration which, until recently, dominated organized military religion? Is Episcopalianism merely the religion of a special social stratum which produced men who sought professional careers in the military establishment? Religious symbolism is found in many aspects of military life, in part because of the danger of death. But the Episcopalian doctrine with its strong emphasis on authority, ceremony, and mission, supplies a positive religion for the military profession. Thus, in the catechism of the Episcopalian Church it is written: "To submit myself to all my governors, teachers, spiritual pastors and masters . . . to order myself lowly and reverently to all my betters and to do my duty in that state of life into which it shall please God to call me."[30]

Because of the religious distribution in his sample, Janowitz was unable to test this implied hypothesis. The population group of this study was somewhat more balanced in terms of religion; Question 63 asked, "What is your religion?", and gave five alter-

30. Janowitz, *The Professional Soldier*, p. 99.

Table 46

EXPERIENCE WITH GOVERNMENT RESEARCH CONTRACTS AND
REFUSAL OF CONTRACTS FOR MORAL OR POLITICAL REASONS

	Yes*	No*	Significance Level
Techniques for staging military coup in U.S.	53%	80%	.001
Establishment of Doomsday Machine by U.S.	53	74	.02
Strategy for combating revolution in U.S. with nuclear weapons	42	69	.001
Technique for starting catalytic war between the Soviet Union and China	37	74	.001
Techniques and utility of preventive war launched by U.S.	26	65	.001
Techniques for violating existing arms control agreement by U.S.	25	65	.001
Techniques for violating prospective agreement on complete and general disarmament by U.S.	20	60	.001
Unilateral disarmament by U.S.	33	34	NS
No government contract would be refused for political or moral reasons	17	6	.01
Establishment of world government	8	8	.20
Other:			
Other similar examples	7	13	.08
Other responses suggesting that, though the question is badly phrased and does not get at real issues, there are moral considerations to be taken into consideration	19	2	.001
(Number)	(81)	(88)	

* As response to question "Have you ever worked on a government research contract in the area of nuclear strategy and disarmament?"

native choices: Protestant, Catholic, Jewish, None, and Other. No significant differences were found among these groups. This was also true when government research was controlled for. Religion may play a part in reinforcing the role of the professional military, but it does not do so for the private nuclear strategists.

Table 46 shows the differences between those individuals who had worked on government research contracts and those who had not. The differences are obvious. On seven of the nine hypothetical contracts, those who had worked on government research contracts were less unwilling to work on them; in all seven cases the difference was significant above the .05 level, and in six of the seven it was above .001. The two exceptions were again our two "left-wing" alternatives, unilateral disarmament and world government; in both instances there was little difference between the two groups.

Once again, the difference over unilateral disarmament was more serious than that over world government. The latter retained its position as the least unfavored hypothetical contract; the former was ranked fifth by those who had done government research and eighth by those who had not. In fact, this statement underestimates the degree of differences; among those who had not worked on a government research contract, seven of the nine hypothetical contracts were rejected by at least 60 percent. Unilateral disarmament, on the other hand, was rejected by only 34 percent; this difference was not reflected among those who had done government research.

It should be noted that, with the exception of unilateral disarmament, both groups ranked the nine hypothetical contracts in about the same way. The difference was that those who had done government research work were much less unwilling to do work in all of these areas. Similarly, 19 percent of those who had done government research stated that they felt that the question had not touched upon the real moral issues. The obvious conclusion is that the two groups have different ethical systems and that the question was phrased in the terms of the respondents who had not done government research, although it is somewhat weakened by the lack of difference on the unilateral disarmament and world government alternatives.

Thus a major weakness in the questionnaire was disclosed. Our personal interviews were directed at this gap, both by interviewing mainly individuals who had done government research and by concentrating upon their attitudes toward morality and responsibility in the area. The interviews were illuminating, since they allowed open-ended questions and pursuit of obscure points. It was concluded that those interviewees who had done government research seemed to have a "situation ethic."[31] Each individual has the responsibility to judge every situation on its own merits in terms of his inner moral commitment rather than external fixed rules. They thus tended to react against the question, since it implied such rules and gave them insufficient data on which to reach a decision. Given ethical problems of the complexity discussed earlier, this is perhaps a logical development. It puts the burden of decision upon each individual. One implication is that, with very few exceptions, these individuals did have a deep moral commitment. In fact, there was a feeling among some of those interviewed that there was actually a moral consensus; consequently there was no point in discussing the issue. Other respondents were dubious of this idea; they argued that though everyone may *say* they value the same things, their actions belie their words.

Despite this difference, there was general agreement among those interviewed that the issue is not discussed among strategists, that nothing would be gained from such discussions, and that the moral debate centered around Herman Kahn had not seriously affected the strategists. They felt that it is almost impossible to change a person's moral attitudes by external pres-

31. For three discussions of this concept from different viewpoints, see Joseph Fletcher, *Situation Ethics: The New Morality* (Philadelphia: Westminster Press, 1966); Jean-Paul Sartre, *Existentialism*, trans. Bernard Frechtman (New York: Philosophical Library, Inc., 1947), especially pp. 26–33; and John A. T. Robinson, *Honest to God* (Philadelphia: Westminster Press, 1963), pp. 105–21.

sure or persuasion. In this sense they seemed to agree with Anatol Rapoport's oft-misinterpreted comment that there can be no true debate between individuals with different opinions on the basic issues of strategy and disarmament.[32] It was felt that discussion of moral issues only angers people without changing them; thus it seems more practical to work within a moral consensus, real or imagined. There seems to be an analogy to American politics, where people can support the same policies for different reasons. A graphic example was the test-ban treaty, which was supported by various individuals because it was a first step to disarmament and world government, a stabilization of the strategic balance, a way to keep the Soviet Union in a position of strategic inferiority, and a minor propaganda ploy in the Cold War.

One respondent, a prominent member of one of the best-known nonprofit research institutes, set forth an alternative set of moral considerations at some length in a personal interview. He contended that the crucial issue was the relationship between the researcher and his client, and that this relationship had two aspects: (1) the researcher does not sell his soul for the client's money, and (2) the researcher works for the interests of the client rather than simply taking his money and doing work that has no real relevance to the client. Presumably, this commitment to the interests of the client allows for a certain amount of redefinition by the policy analyst, as in the Wohlstetter-RAND bases study, which began with the question of location of new strategic air bases and wound up dealing with the whole question of vulnerability of strategic forces.[33]

32. Anatol Rapoport, "The Armers and the Disarmers," *Nation* 196 (March 2, 1968), 175–77, 188; see also his "Strategic and Non-Strategic Approaches to Problems of Security and Peace" and especially his subsequent debate with Albert Wohlstetter in Kathleen Archibald, ed., *Strategic Interaction and Conflict: Original Papers and Discussion*, International Security Program, Institute of International Studies, University of California (Berkeley, Calif., 1966), pp. 88–102, 107–34.

33. Smith, "Strategic Expertise and National Security Policy."

This is, in fact, the classic code of ethics of the private professional such as the lawyer or the physician. A recent study of applied social science in government, which uses international security as a case study, is also based on the client-researcher relationship.[34] It should be noted that this is not identical to Posvar's suggestion that the interest of the state should be put above all else, although the two may coincide. On the other hand, it is at least questionable whether this concern for the interest of the client is appropriate when dealing with nuclear strategy and disarmament. If the horse cavalry had hired a policy analyst to study its problems of modernization in the nuclear age, would he have had a primary obligation to his client or to some concept of the national interest? One solution would be to recommend they trade their horses for helicopters; but what if the researcher knew that this advice, although quite sound, would be rejected by the client? Thus the question of responsibility and strategy blend.

Posvar has suggested that civilians doing government research may have taken the nonpolitical stance of the professional military for its own.

The whole study of civil-military relations, through their domestic emphasis, may have had (a) misleading effect on strategy . . . , in that it may conceal the need for political perspective on the part of the strategist. . . . The injunction against his taking part in any political activity is easily extended to become a sanction against his taking interest in or account of political considerations as they affect strategy. For the military man, who is strongly impressed by the argument for objective civilian control, professionalism may seem to require his limiting the scope of his perceptions to the technical aspect of his task. The civilian strategy expert, who is schooled in scientific methods and who has a predilection for visualizing problems in technical terms, is willing enough to follow suit. Even if he is not deterred by what he regards as his principles from an examination of the political factors which are inherent in his work, he may be bored by them. So the military professionals who are the subjects of objective civilian

34. Archibald, *Social Conflict*, especially chap. 6.

control and the civilian experts who are the agents of subjective civilian control may be alike in their disdain for political perspectives.[35]

Indeed, an examination of Tables 45 and 46 indicates that the ex-military group and those who had worked on government research contracts can be grouped together against those who had not worked on such contracts, supporting Posvar's hypothesis. There were two other questions related to this idea; both were statements with seven-point agree-disagree scale responses. Question 46 read:

Civilians studying strategy and disarmament have tended to stress technical analysis and to ignore political problems.

Of the sample, 55 percent agreed with the statement, and 40 percent disagreed. Only 40 percent of those who had worked on government research contracts agreed, as compared with 70 percent of those who had not done such work; the difference was significant at the .001 level.

Question 49 read:

Civilians outside of government who are working in the area of strategy and disarmament have been too much concerned with making the present international system more tolerable rather than exploring ways to change the system itself.

Forty-nine percent of the sample agreed, and 40 percent disagreed (N was 158). Of those who had done government research, 32 percent agreed; the comparable figure for those who had not was 65 percent; once again the difference was significant at the .001 level. Strictly speaking, this does not prove our hypothesis; it only indicates that the two groups had different views of the current situation in the study of strategy and disarmament. However, considering the magnitude of the differences and on the assumption that the two groups were observing roughly the same

35. "Strategy Expertise and National Security," pp. 273–74.

phenomena, it does not seem unreasonable to conclude that those who had not worked on government research contracts were more interested in the political aspects of strategy and disarmament than those who had. It will be remembered that a similar pattern appeared in the earlier study of motivation, where those who had worked on government research had been less influenced by strong policy motives than those who had not done such work.[36]

There seemed to be a major split between those who had done government research with intellectual motives and technical orientations and those who had not done such work and were more concerned with the political aspects of strategy. The two groups were roughly equal in size, which increased the significance of the division. Unfortunately there is no way of knowing whether there is a causal relationship between doing government research and lack of interest in political considerations, much less its direction. It is interesting to speculate whether only individuals without strong political interest are able to obtain government research contracts or whether the process of doing such work socializes the individual to the prevailing viewpoint. No doubt the particular mixture varies with the individual; however, if the data on motivation for entering the field are to be trusted, the former process would seem to be the more important. If so, this suggests that one channel of influence, government research contracts, has been unused by those most interested in the political aspects of strategy. This is not too surprising, since the government agencies who grant such contracts are presumably not interested in making major political changes. Also, there are other channels of influence which may be effective, such as the public strategic debate, direct political action, or personally influencing individuals doing government research. Since there is no information on the relative efficacy of various channels for various tasks, it is not possible to estimate how much difference this restriction makes; nevertheless, it does not seem to be a particularly desirable state of affairs.

36. See above, pp. 65–67.

views and prospects

In this chapter an attempt will be made to look at the future development of the study of nuclear strategy and disarmament by civilians outside the government. Little data on the subject was produced from the questionnaire, so the discussion will be necessarily speculative. First let us consider the present status of the field, and then examine its likely future development in several areas.

the present pause

The study of nuclear strategy and disarmament is currently in a hiatus. This can be clearly seen in the dependence of current analysis upon the basic concepts formulated in the late 1950s and early 1960s. The exact dates involved are controversial. One respondent, with excellent access to classified materials, said that, with the partial exception of escalation, the basic elements of current strategic thought had been set forth by 1956. However, these theories did not really surface publicly until about 1957. Between 1957 and 1961 Henry Kissinger, Albert Wohlstetter, Bernard Brodie, Herman Kahn, and Thomas Schelling published seminal works.[1] The concept of stable deterrence through mutual invulnerable second-strike forces was established during this time. Essentially we are still living off this intellectual capital.

Most of the work in nuclear strategy and disarmament since this time can be divided into repetition and elaboration of these ideas, attacks upon them, and their translation into policy. The last was an especially exciting area. With the election of John Kennedy as president, his appointment of Robert McNamara as secretary of defense, and the establishment of the Arms Control and Disarmament Agency (ACDA), civilians outside of government were brought into government to change these ideas into policy.

The current pause in the field is apparent in several ways. There was a tendency for respondents, especially those working primarily in nuclear strategy and disarmament, to look back at the early 1960s as a "golden age," when exciting things were happening. There was a general feeling that the intellectual action is no longer in nuclear strategy and disarmament. Some of the major figures in the field either seem to be bogged down and repeating themselves or are leaving the area. Some respondents, especially those in the research institutes and private corporations, said that they were really interested in developing a policy science; they viewed nuclear weapons policy as the first major subject field in which their methodology had been applied, but

---

1. Kissinger, *Nuclear Weapons and Foreign Policy*; Albert J. Wohlstetter, "The Delicate Balance of Terror," *Foreign Affairs* 38 (1959), 211–34; Brodie, *Strategy in the Missile Age*; Kahn, *On Thermonuclear War*; Thomas C. Schelling and Morton H. Halperin, *Strategy and Arms Control* (New York: Twentieth Century Fund, 1961). See also Schelling, *The Strategy of Conflict*; despite the publication date of this volume (1963), the bulk of the book is composed of articles originally published before 1960.

their interest was in the methodology rather than the subject. There was a general feeling of "what next?"

At least three reasons for this change are apparent: the natural trend of intellectual progress, the triumph of the basic idea of stable deterrence through mutual invulnerable second-strike forces, and the Vietnam War. We shall examine each separately.

The course of intellectual change is unlikely to run smooth. Rather, it seems to occur in concentrated bursts of creativity, followed by periods of digestion and dissemination. If the change is a major one, the subsequent hiatus is likely to be correspondingly long, unless the process is disrupted by external events. It is easy to overlook the difficulty of people changing their basic frame of reference; there is a good deal of truth to the theory that it only happens when one generation dies out and is replaced by another. Indeed, one of the major problems of the nuclear age may be that our weapons change faster than our ideas of what to do with them. The change in perspective involved in the acceptance of the idea of mutual second-strike forces was considerable. The current pause is thus to some extent a logical event.

A second reason for this pause has been that the basic idea of stable deterrence through mutual invulnerable second-strike forces was accepted quite rapidly, not only by many of the private nuclear strategists, but also by the American government. Indeed, the ideas no sooner became public than they seemed to become government policy. This acceptance was due in large part to the coincidence that, just as the ideas were being made public, a new administration came into office in Washington. It was a Democratic one; hence its contacts with intellectuals, including those working in nuclear strategy and disarmament, were considerably better than a comparable Republican administration's contacts would have been. Since it was replacing an administration of the opposite party, it had an interest in altering nuclear weapons policy; more precisely, it was somewhat less unwilling to make changes, in concept as well as in policy. Thus the idea was accepted and translated into policy remarkably rapidly. (In the process it may have given some of the private nuclear strategists an exaggerated view of their political prowess, which may lead to frustration if a similar future theoretical development does not coincide so well with political factors.) The danger of the process, of course, was that it was quite possible that the new ideas would become a new dogma, which might in turn become outmoded.

It is also significant that the acceptance of this idea implied a stable situation. This was not inherent in the idea itself; it was rather the product of a combination of ideas and technology. Wohlstetter, after all, titled his article "The Delicate Balance Of Terror"; given the technology of the time, it seemed delicate indeed. However, the development of hardened solid-fuel intercontinental ballistic missiles, combined with the Polaris-type missile submarine, meant that a mutual invulnerable second-strike situation could be achieved without much extra effort by the United States (and, presumably, by the Soviet Union). There was some question as to whether we could safely cross the intervening time period (this was the basis of the missile gap controversy); however, once both sides had accumulated respectable stockpiles of these weapons in the 1960s, there seemed to be nothing more to do in the area of nuclear strategy. Nuclear disarmament remained an open question, but the achievement of stable deterrence removed much of its urgency, at least in the short run. However, all of this was susceptible to changes in technology, as all of the major authors realized; as we shall see, there are suggestions that these changes may be upon us.

Perhaps the most obvious reason for the intellectual pause in nuclear weapons policy theory is the Vietnam War. It has been argued, particularly by those interested in arms control and disarmament, that the war has slowed the adoption of new steps in these areas because the American government is concentrating on the war to the exclusion of everything else, Congress will not approve any measures that appear to help our enemies, and Russia cannot afford to seem friendly to the United States. It is difficult to evaluate this argument; however, the fact that Soviet-American talks on strategic arms limitation have gone on with some chance of success suggests that it can be overstated.

The fact is that those interested in arms control and disarmament had trouble deciding what should follow the test-ban treaty, even before the Vietnam fighting escalated to its present level.

The effects of the war are clearer in two other ways. In the first place, it has caused a considerable diversion of talent from nuclear weapons policy. As long as the United States was not involved in a shooting war, the strategic community naturally tended to concentrate on nuclear policy because of the obvious magnitude of the stakes involved. However, Vietnam has brought many of these same people into areas such as counterinsurgency, logistics, and conventional weapons technology. Much of this is due to a natural shift in concern by the government; research institutes and corporations, which exist because of government research contracts, must naturally tailor their proposals to fit the problems in which the government is interested. One well-known example is the evaluation by the RAND Corporation of the interrogation of Vietcong prisoners.

A second effect of Vietnam has been to remove much of the public pressure on the American government to alter its nuclear weapons policies, particularly in regard to further steps in arms control and disarmament. There is a good deal of inertia in defense policy; change normally comes only from the pressure of external events. Although national actions in the international arena are probably the major determinant, the impact of a concerned and articulate public should not be discounted. However, many people who were formerly concerned about nuclear policy have shifted their attention to Vietnam.

If these are the causes of the current hiatus in the study of nuclear strategy and disarmament, what are its effects? It is by no means obvious that it is a bad thing, although our respondents tended to view it as such. We have noted that it is in part a natural reaction to the creativity of the 1950s and early 1960s. It has given those who are interested an opportunity to disseminate the basic concepts of deterrence more widely among an attentive public, a matter to which we shall return later. Some of the elaboration has been useful. Translating theory into government policy inevitably takes time; the pause has allowed the latter to catch up with the former. Nor is it inherently bad to rely upon well-established ideas; there are those who contend that not only has nothing new been said in philosophy since Plato and Aristotle but that the intervening years have been a decline because we have drawn away from the original sources.

However, the terms *pause* and *hiatus* imply that the phenomenon is felt by me to be a temporary one and that a renewal of intellectual effort in the field is to be expected. This is, of course, something of a matter of faith. Yet the problems involved are so complex and important, and the current solutions so limited, that it is difficult to doubt that new ideas will be needed in the foreseeable future.

If we are indeed in a temporary pause, the question of when it will end becomes important. For, though this state may be healthy, it can have unfortunate consequences if it becomes too prolonged. This is most likely to happen if external events require policy changes but we are unable to overcome the inertia of defense decision-making. Indeed, there was a general feeling of concern among many of the respondents about this problem in Washington today. We have already noted that the present apparently stable situation is subject to alteration by technological change.

This change seems to have arrived with the almost simultaneous development of multiple, independent warheads for intercontinental missiles (MIRV) and the antiballistic missile (ABM). These two systems offer, at least in principle, the possibility of overturning the strategic balance, which was founded on the invulnerability and effectiveness of solid-fueled missiles. These technological developments have already produced a considerable literature and debate,[2] and there is no end in sight. We seem therefore on the eve of the next major state in the postwar strategic debate.

2. Among the more recent literature on these topics are: Ralph E. Lapp, *Arms beyond Doubt: The Tyranny of Weapons Technology* (New York:

the future: supply and demand

Will the private nuclear strategists continue to exist? Or have they simply been a short-run phenomenon within the strategic community, substituting until the government can replace them with in-house expertise? There are two aspects to this question, which we may call supply and demand: whether there will be individuals prepared to work in the field and whether there will be any demand for their services. The data of this study, naturally, are more relevant to the problem of supply, since demand is determined by people outside of its population; however, we may essay some answers in both areas.

As far as supply is concerned, at the most elementary level the questions about the percentage of professional time spent in the study of strategy and disarmament five years ago, today, and five years in the future suggested only a very small decline in the individuals working in the field, one that could easily be made up by people entering the area. Somewhat more indirect indicators confirmed this picture of a constant supply of private nuclear strategists in the future. The fact that younger members of the sample were more academically oriented suggests that the field is acquiring qualifications for expertise like other areas of study; this, in turn, seems likely to make it more stable over the long run.

Similarly, the tendency of younger individuals to be more motivated by intellectual rather than policy motives should make recruitment less dependent upon the current political situation.

Cowles Educational Books, Inc., 1970); American Security Council, National Strategy Committee, *U.S.S.R. Vs. U.S.A.: The ABM and the Changed Strategic Balance,* 2d ed. (Washington: Acropolis Books, 1969); Johan J. Holst and William Schneider, Jr., *Why ABM? Policy Issues in the Missile Defense Controversy* (New York: Pergamon Press, Inc., 1969); Center for the Study of Democratic Institutions, *Anti-ballistic Missile: Yes or No?* (New York: Hill & Wang, 1969); Abram Chayes and Jerome B. Wiesner, *ABM: An Evaluation of the Decision to Deploy an Anti-ballistic Missile System* (New York: Harper & Row, 1969). As this listing indicates, the ABM has received more attention, although MIRV may be more damaging to the strategic balance.

The development of strategy and disarmament within political science means that it can be fitted into the academic framework without the difficulty of establishing a new discipline, or even a new interdisciplinary area. Finally, the fact that most of the sample had little interest in teaching, although not without its unfortunate aspects, implies that despite intellectual motives most private strategists will retain a high level of interest in policy questions. The evidence available thus suggests that the supply of private nuclear strategists will not decrease significantly over time.

The question of demand is somewhat more complicated. However, one interesting piece of evidence that it is becoming stable is a developing division of labor within the strategic community, in which the private nuclear strategist has an important role to play. The private civilian strategists, who have developed practically all of the strategic concepts since World War II, carry on a continuing debate over the major issues in nuclear strategy and disarmament. This debate, which may be called the *strategic* debate, is carried on partly in public (increasingly so in recent years) and partly within and between government agencies. In the latter segment of the field, the government research contract is the key that brings the private strategist temporarily inside of government.

From this debate, certain concepts tend to emerge as prominent solutions, to use Schelling's term. This, in turn, gives rise to a second level of debate, the translation of these concepts into policy. In this *policy* debate, the other two groups within the strategic community hold dominant positions. The professional military man speaks as the practitioner, the one who must put the ideas into operation. As such, he rightly demands and receives a major voice in the debate. The government official's role may vary with the individual personality. However, he normally represents the rest of the government within the debate; thus he is often responsible for introducing factors such as the budget or public opinion. One of the drawbacks of the system is that he often also tends to be responsible for bringing in political, as opposed to military, questions; if he is not inclined to do so, they may never be raised.

The private strategist has a subsidiary role in the policy debate; his entry is controlled by the other two groups. In contrast to the strategic debate, the private strategist's influence here, if any, is necessarily indirect; he usually does research for either the professional military or government officials. (There is a potential conflict of interest here because the private strategist can work for either or both competitive groups; among others the RAND Corporation was faced with the problem.[3] The result has tended to be that particular institutes have become informally linked with individual services or departments. Examples are the Research Analysis Corporation and the army, the Center for Naval Analysis and the navy, RAND and the air force, and the Institute for Defense Analyses and the Department of Defense.)[4] In the process of doing this research, the private strategist may have an opportunity to change his client's position somewhat, if he wishes to do so.[5]

It seems unlikely that this system will change radically in the foreseeable future. The private strategist continues to possess both expertise and available time, making him a valuable ally in the policy debate. Nor is there any sign that other groups of the strategic community are prepared to take over the strategic debate, despite occasional exhortations for them to do so.[6]

Probably the most vulnerable facet of the private strategist's role is that of government research, since it is entirely outside of his control. A change of administration, or even of personnel within a government department, can completely cut off an individual or an institute from access to government. As yet we have

3. Smith, *RAND Corporation*, pp. 125–39.

4. Lyons and Morton, *Schools for Strategy*, pp. 240–57.

5. A useful discussion of this process is Kathleen Archibald on the "strategic" orientation of the social scientist (*Social Conflict*, chap. 6).

6. An example is Colonel Robert N. Ginsburgh, "The Challenge to Military Professionalism," *Foreign Affairs* 42 (1964), 255-68.

had inadequate experience with such changes to be specific about their effects, but they clearly could be very important.

The problem is especially acute for the research institutes and those private corporations who are deeply involved in such work; without government contracts, they cannot survive. Although some are attempting to branch out and find other customers, there is still no substitute for the federal government when it comes to funding major research projects in strategy and disarmament. It is entirely possible that there will be some rather severe weeding-out of institutes and corporations over the next few years. However, it is unlikely that the basic pattern will change much in the foreseeable future. To do in-house the work now contracted for outside would require an immense increase in the government bureaucracy of a kind that few are likely to advocate, at least not as long as the quality of the contract work remains reasonably high. Although it will undoubtedly have its ups and downs, the government research contract in nuclear strategy and disarmament seems here to stay.

Another indicator of stability is the academic tendency of the younger members of the sample; along with the development of the field into a specialty area within political science, this suggests that the university may increasingly provide an institution of refuge in short-run decreases of government interest. The university-based scholar is in a much better position vis-à-vis the government as far as survival is concerned, although he too must gain access, especially to the policy debate. Thus even if the research institutes were eliminated, the universities would retain a cadre interested in the area who could be activated later if government interest was renewed.

the teaching imperative

The civilian strategist at a university, however, must expect eventually to have to do some teaching as well as research. The sample had not shown much interest in college teaching. This may be because the field is relatively young. One respondent compared it to Slavic studies, which until a few years ago had relatively little interest for teachers, at least partly because its members were young enough not to be enthusiastic about creating competitors for themselves. However, this has apparently changed with the general development of the field; a similar transformation may come in strategy and disarmament.

Teaching is an area where future developments may be important. It takes place at two levels: graduate training to produce professional colleagues and general education for the undergraduate. We are concerned here with the latter.

Nuclear strategy and disarmament is going to be a major public issue for a long time. The magnitude of the stakes involved probably ensures this; what makes it a certainty is the tremendous amounts of money involved. This in turn brings in Congress; given deep involvement by both Congress and the executive, the issues are bound to be the subject of public debate. Moreover, it is likely that major decisions will have to be made by the government on policy in this field. Regardless of whether the ABM debate escalates to this level, it is unlikely that technological and political change will pass the field by.

If we can expect public debate over issues of strategy and disarmament that may affect the decisions of the government, it is important that at least the attentive public be as well informed as possible about the subject. It is strange that an individual is not considered fully educated unless he has some grasp of the basic concepts of economics affecting his living standard but that there is no concern about understanding the concepts of deterrence, which may determine whether he lives or dies. This process of enlightenment operates on at least two levels. The public nature of much of the strategic debate means that an interested observer can keep up with the field rather easily. However, this should be supplemented by making undergraduate courses in strategy and disarmament available at most major colleges and universities.

As we have seen, this will probably be done within the framework of the discipline of political science rather than the inter-disciplinary program, which might seem the logical alternative.[7] This has certain concrete administrative advantages; it is much easier to add a course to an existing department than to establish a new program. One promising approach is to link a semester course in foreign policy with one in strategy and deterrence. This process is simplified by the fact that one product of the current hiatus in the study of strategy and disarmament has been a series of books, both basic texts and readers, either specifically designed or quite suitable for such courses;[8] they will be particularly useful at schools with inadequate library resources.

The potential long-term impact on policy of education in strategy and disarmament can be great. More importantly, its absence might have very unfortunate consequences. Regardless of our individual attitudes toward the public debate of strategic issues, we have a responsibility to do what we can to keep it as well informed and relevant as possible. If we do not and if the public pressures the government to take irresponsible actions, we cannot hold ourselves blameless.

american democracy and the private nuclear strategists

At the conclusion of this study at least three questions must be asked, although the answers cannot be as confident as we should like. How much influence do the private nuclear strategists have in American governmental desisions? In what direction is this influence exerted? What are the implications for American democracy of the monopoly of expertise by a small group in matters concerning the life and death of our civilization?

7. See pp. 91–102, "The Dominance of Political Science."

8. See for example Morton H. Halperin, *Contemporary Military Strategy* (Boston: Little, Brown & Co., 1966); Morton Berkowitz and Peter G. Bock, eds., *American National Security* (New York: The Free Press, 1965); Wesley W. Posvar et al., eds., *American Defense Policy* (Baltimore: Johns Hopkins University Press, 1965); and Davis B. Bobrow, ed., *Components of Defense Policy* (Chicago: Rand McNally & Co., 1965).

Because of the nature of the study, the amount of influence the private nuclear strageists have had on American policy in strategy and disarmament cannot be determined; respondents included only the private nuclear strategists themselves. Another study, involving both the strategists and the government officials supposedly influenced by them, might provide data in this area.[9] We have noted that the strategists seemed to *feel* that they have had considerable influence; more than a third felt that as individuals they had significantly influenced a policy of the United States government in strategy and disarmament, and over one-half said that civilians not employed by government had influenced American defense policy either "a good deal" or "very much." There is, however, no way of judging whether this is a correct impression.

As a working hypothesis for another study, this author would suggest that the private nuclear strategists overstate their influence in specific decisions, although their influence at the more general level of strategic thinking has indeed been considerable. This hypothesis is based upon a few interviews with individuals who are private nuclear strategists but who have also worked in government; one observed that he had never heard anyone in government even use the name of one of the group. The hypothesis is supported by an admittedly cursory examination of the memoirs and biographies of prominent figures in the Eisenhower and Kennedy administrations.[10] The indexes of these books were

9. A study along these lines, although with a much more limited scope, is being conducted by the Bureau of Social Science Research, Inc., in Washington; it is concerned with the influence of social science research on air force planning.

10. Dwight D. Eisenhower, *Mandate for Change, 1953–1956* (Garden City, N.Y.: Doubleday & Co., 1963) and *Waging Peace, 1956–1961* (Garden City, N.Y.: Doubleday & Co., 1965); Robert J. Donovan, *Eisenhower: The Inside Story* (New York: Harper & Bros., 1956); John Robinson Neal, *John Foster Dulles: A Biography* (New York: Harper & Bros., 1957); Emmet John Hughes, *The Ordeal of Power: A Political Memoir of the Eisenhower Years* (New York: Atheneum Press, 1963); Malcolm E. Jewell, *Senatorial Politics and Foreign Policy* (Lexington: University of Kentucky

checked for references to the two individuals whom the sample felt had made the most significant contributions to the field (Herman Kahn and Thomas Schelling) and to the best-known organization in the area, the RAND Corporation. Only the Schlesinger book has *any* references to these three (two to RAND and two to Schelling). We would hypothesize, then, that the private strategists have overstated their specific influence, although they do seem to have done better under the Kennedy administration than under Eisenhower.

There was no expectation of discussing the policy positions of the sample as a whole; such discussion of a group that includes representatives of practically every political and strategic view in America seemed pointless. The policy links between Robert Strausz-Hupe, Edward Teller, Herman Kahn, Hans Bethe, Kenneth Boulding, Linus Pauling, and A. J. Muste are obscure, to say the least. There are no comparable data for control groups outside of the population, and the instruments themselves were quite crude and did not measure many essential distinctions in such attitudes (as many of the sample informed us). Nevertheless, there is one unexpected uniformity that should be noted. Both on motives and policy attitudes, *the sample was much more concerned about the threat of nuclear weapons than about communism.* This is true even though the sample was dominated by political scientists, whom most respondents that were interviewed regarded as being more "hard-line" than other disciplines.

Press, 1962); Robert Cutler, *No Time for Rest* (Boston: Little, Brown & Co., 1966); Menlo J. Pusey, *Eisenhower the President* (New York: Macmillan Co., 1956); Theodore C. Sorensen, *Kennedy* (New York: Harper & Row, 1965); and Arthur M. Schlesinger, Jr., *A Thousand Days: John F. Kennedy in the White House* (Boston: Houghton Mifflin Co., 1965). Three books were excluded because their authors were members of the study population: Roger Hilsman, *To Move a Nation: The Politics of Foreign Policy in the Administration of John F. Kennedy* (Garden City, N.Y.: Doubleday & Co., 1967); James M. Gavin, *War and Peace in the Space Age* (New York: Harper & Bros., 1958); and Maxwell D. Taylor, *The Uncertain Trumpet* (New York: Harper & Bros., 1959). The Hilsman work has one reference to Kahn and three to RAND; the Gavin and Taylor indexes do not contain mention of any of the three items.

Whether one approves of this tendency or not obviously depends on one's own policy preferences. At any rate, to repeat an earlier observation, the sample as a whole seemed unpromising material for a nuclear anticommunist crusade, despite its many internal differences on quite basic issues.

There is something repugnant about the idea of a relatively small number of people having a virtual monopoly of an expertise whose application may decide whether our civilization survives. The problem is further complicated by the lack of political accountability and indirect responsibility of the private nuclear strategist. One may well ask whether such a situation is compatible with American democratic ideals.

However, as we have seen in our discussion of professionalization, a monopoly of socially vital expertise is not an unprecedented phenomenon, even in the area of violence. In a complex world one can no more expect a majority of Americans to be experts on nuclear weapons policy than on law, medicine, or economics. Our concern then shifts to two particular areas. The first is the *quality* of the advice of the private nuclear strategists —that is, whether they will produce, or at least not hinder, government policies that will enable the United States to survive. At its simplest, this can be tested by deciding whether the government policies are right or wrong. At a somewhat more complicated level, each particular decision seems likely to involve a different group of individuals, presenting a research problem of staggering complexity. Perhaps there is no solution short of simply deciding whether one approves of government policy in strategy and disarmament.

Another consideration, however, is that this "good" policy be produced without destroying our democratic institutions. Although survival is a useful minimal goal, we can also prefer not to pay the price of a "garrison state" form of government. One obvious conclusion of this study is that the unity between "specialists in violence" seems to be largely mythical, judging from our sample's competitive attitudes toward the professional military. Another obvious feature of the private nuclear strategists is their general openness. Ninety percent of the sample disagreed with the statement that strategy should be controlled by the experts, a remarkable example of consensus. Moreover, corporateness is low, as measured by respondents' attitude toward an "establishment" and the lack of any prescribed recruiting mechanism. A third piece of evidence is that one need not even work full time in the area to be considered influential. This openness makes it difficult to view the private nuclear strategists as a conspiratorial group preparing to unite with the military and take over the country, either deliberately or in a fit of absent-mindedness. The policies of the strategic community may or may not save American democracy; their role in the policy process seems unlikely to seriously threaten it.

11. The classic formulation of this question is Harold D. Lasswell, "The Garrison State," *American Journal of Sociology* 46 (1941), 455–68, and "The Garrison State Today," in Samuel P. Huntington, ed., *Changing Patterns of Military Politics* (New York: Free Press of Glencoe, 1962), pp. 51–70.

sources of the
master bibliography

There were four different types of principal sources for the master bibliography: bibliographies; periodical indexes; material from the Armed Services Technical Information Agency; and publication lists from various organizations and institutes. Each will be discussed in turn.

bibliographies

Because of their number, periodical articles in these bibliographies were not included; the only source for periodical articles were the periodical indexes discussed in the next section. Ninety-one bibliographies used are listed below. (Two were loaned to me in confidence.)

Basic, Brief Bibliography on Disarmament Issues. Disarmament Information Committee, American Association for the United Nations. New York, 1964.

Bibliography of Pamphlets and Books on Peace and International Affairs. Peace Education and Action through the Churches, American Friends Service Committee. Philadelphia, n.d.

Bowman, Albert. *Peace and Militarization: A Survey of Current Documents and Reports.* List No. 1. U.S. Committee against Militarization. Chicago, 1950

Books and Pamphlets. Turn toward Peace. New York, n.d.

Books and Pamphlets on Peace, Nonviolence, Reconciliation. Fellowship of Reconciliation. Nyack, N.Y., n.d.

Books on Proliferation of Nuclear Weapons. Turn toward Peace. New York, 1965.

Brief Bibliography on Disarmament and Modern War. National Committee for a Sane Nuclear Policy. New York, n.d.

Brief Bibliography on Nuclear Testing, Fallout & Radiation. National Committee for a Sane Nuclear Policy. New York, n.d.

Brinton, Ellen Starr, and Hiram Doty. *Guide to the Swarthmore College Collection: A Memorial to Jane Addams.* Peace Collection Publication No. 1, Swarthmore College. Swarthmore, Pa., 1947.

Brody, Richard A. "Deterrence Strategies: An Annotated Bibliography." *Journal of Conflict Resolution* IV (December, 1960), 443–57.

Brown, Noel J. "The Moral Problem of Modern Warfare: A Bibliography." In *Morality and Modern Warfare: The State of the Question.* Edited by William J. Nagle. Baltimore: Helicon Press, 1960.

Cary, Mary G. *Some Basic Readings on Problems of Peace and Non-Violence.* Friends Peace Committee. Philadelphia, 1956.

Civil-Military Relations: An Annotated Bibliography, 1940–1952. Prepared under the direction of the Committee on Civil-Military Relations Research, Social Science Research Council. New York: Columbia University Press, 1954.

Clemens, Walter C., Jr. *Soviet Disarmament Policy, 1917–1963.* Hoover Institution Bibliographical Series XXII, Hoover Institution on War, Revolution, and Peace, Stanford University. Stanford, Calif., 1965.

Coward, H. Roberts. *A Selected Bibliography on Arms Control and Related Problems.* ACDA Regional No. 1, C/63-7, Center for International Studies, Massachusetts Institute of Technology. Cambridge, Mass., 1963.

Craig, Hardin, Jr. *A Bibliography of Encyclopedias and Dictionaries Dealing with Military, Naval, and Maritime Affairs, 1577–1961.* 2d ed. Fondren Library, Rice University. Houston, Tex., 1962.

Crawford, Elisabeth T. *The Social Sciences in International and Military Policy: An Analytic Bibliography.* AFOSR 65-1890, Bureau of Social Science Research, Inc. Washington, D.C., 1965.

Crum, Norman J. *Arms Control Guide: An Annotated Bibliography with Glossary, Directory, Biographies, Proposals, and Research.* SP-215, TEMPO, General Electric Company. Santa Barbara, Calif., 1963.

Current Thoughts on Peace and War.

David, Robert H.; P. B. Carpenter; W. M. Cannon; R. R. Gilliam; and C. W. Missler. *Arms Control Simulation.* TM-(L)-633, System Development Corporation. Santa Monica, Calif., 1961.

Defense and Disarmament: A Bibliography of Current Literature. Rev. ed. Canadian Institute of International Affairs. Toronto, 1963.

"Disarmament: A Bibliography." *Survival* VI (January-February, 1960), pp. 38–40.

Disarmament and Arms Control. Committee for World Development and World Disarmament. New York, n.d.

Educational Resources for a Turn toward Peace. Peace Education Program, New England Region, American Friends Service Committee, as a service to Turn toward Peace. N.p., n.d.

Emme, Eugene M. *National Air Power and International Politics: A Select Bibliography.* Studies and Research Branch, Historical Division, Department of the Air Force Library. Maxwell Air Force Base, Ala., 1950.

Estep, Raymond. *An Air Power Bibliography.* Air University Documentary Research Study AU-252-RSI. Documentary Research Division, Research Studies Institute, Air University. Maxwell Air Force Base, Ala., 1956.

Evans, Barbara D. *Selected Bibliography on the United Nations.* Rev. ed. American Association of University Women. Washington, D.C., 1962.

Fischer, George. *Soviet Disarmament Policy: A Survey of Recent Sources.* C/61-25. Center for International Studies, Massachusetts Institute of Technology. Cambridge, Mass., 1961.

Gitlin, Todd. *Bibliography of War/Peace Books.* Prepared by Students for a Democratic Society for the Liberal Study Group, Fifteenth Annual Congress, United States National Student Association, Columbus, Ohio, August 19–30, 1962.

Hewitt, Vivian D. *Book Check List No. 2: A Selection of Significant Books on Disarmament and Arms Control.* Committee for World Development and World Disarmament. New York, 1964.

Hoggett, David. *Nonviolence and Peacemaking.* Commonweal Trust. London, 1963.

Insurgency and Counterinsurgency in Indonesia. N.p., n.d. Found in Sterling Library, Yale University, New Haven, Conn., 1964.

Insurgency and Counterinsurgency since World War II. N.p., n.d. Found in Sterling Library, Yale University, New Haven, Conn., 1964.

Jensen, Lloyd, "Disarmament and Arms Control: Some of the Recent Literature." *Background* VI (Winter, 1963), 41–47.

Kenworthy, Leonard S. *Free and Inexpensive Materials on World Affairs.* Bureau of Publications, Teachers College, Columbia University. New York, 1963.

Krim, Murray, and Milton Schwebel. "Human Survival: A Selected Bibliography." *American Journal of Orthopsychiatry* XXXIII (January, 1963), 183–91.

Leikind, Morris C. "A Bibliography of Atomic Energy (March 1, 1964–February 1, 1947)." *Bulletin of the Atomic Scientists* III (April-May, 1947), 127–35.

Materials for the Ratification Campaign for the Test-Ban Treaty. National Committee for a Sane Nuclear Policy. New York, n.d.

Miller, William Robert. *Bibliography of Books on War, Pacifism, Non-Violence, and Related Studies.* Rev. ed. Fellowship of Reconciliation. Nyack, N.Y., 1961.

Newcombe, Hanna. *Bibliography on War and Peace.* Peace Research Abstracts, Canadian Peace Research Institute. Dundas, Ont., 1963.

Ney, Col. Virgil (U.S. Army [ret.]). "Guerilla Warfare: Annotated Bibliography." *Military Review* XLI (November, 1961), 97–112.

Peace Books (also entitled *Short Bibliography*). Student Peace Union. New York, n.d.

The Poor Man's Guide to War/Peace Literature. Spring-Summer, 1964. New York Peace Information Center. New York, 1964.

Reason, Barbara; Margaret B. Mughisuddin; and Bum-Joon Lee Park. *Cuba Since Castro: A Bibliography of Relevant Literature.* Special Operations Research Office, American University. Washington, 1962.

Renstrom, Arthur G. *Aeropolitics: A Selective Bibliography on the Influence of Aviation on Society.* Aeronautics Division, Reference Department, Library of Congress. Washington, 1948.

————. *United States Aviation Policy: A Selective Bibliography.* Division of Aeronautics, Library of Congress. Washington, 1947

Scanlon, Helen Lawrence. *Security in the Atomic Age: International Control of the Bomb.* Select Bibliographies, No. 15, Carnegie Endowment for International Peace. Washington, 1946.

Seelye, Mary. *Book Check List: Recent Important Books on Disarmament and Arms Control.* Committee for World Development and World Disarmament. New York, 1962.

Stevenson, Eric, and John Teeple. *Research in Arms Control and Disarmament, 1960–1963.* International Affairs Program, Ford Foundation. New York, 1963.

Suggested Background Reading. Committee for the Application of the Behavioral Sciences to the Strategies of Peace. San Francisco, n.d.

Suggested Bibliography. Mimeographed list found in files of the New York Peace Information Center, New York; apparently a college class reading list, but without identification. It consists of three and one-half pages, but the last page has been torn across an entry, so it may have been longer originally.

Suggestions for a Study Course on Areas of Tensions Leading to International Conflict with Methods for Constructive Reconciliation, and Bibliography. 2d rev. ed. Fellowship of Reconciliation, Los Angeles Office. Los Angeles, Calif., 1963.

Tompkins, Dorothy C. *Civil Defense in the States: A Bibliography.* Defense Bibliographies, No. 3, Bureau of Public Administration, University of California. Berkeley, Calif., 1953.

―――. *National Defense in 1950, The Federal Program: A Selected Bibliography.* Defense Bibliographies, No. 1, Bureau of Public Administration, University of California. Berkeley, Calif., 1950.

―――. *Sabotage and Its Prevention during Wartime.* Defense Bibliographies, No. 2, Bureau of Public Administration, University of California. Berkeley, Calif., 1951.

Triple Revolution Bibliography. American Friends Service Committee, New York, n.d.

United Nations, Department of Political and Security Council Affairs, Atomic Energy Commission Group. *An International Bibliography on Atomic Energy.* Vol. I. *Political, Economic, and Social Aspects.* New York, 1949.

―――. *An International Bibliography on Atomic Energy, Supplement No. 1.* Vol. I. *Political Economic, and Social Aspects.* Lake Success, N.Y., 1950.

U.S. Air Force Academy, Library. *Arms Control.* Special Bibliography Series, No. 20. Colorado Springs, Colo., 1962.

―――. *International Organization and Military Security Systems.* Special Bibliography Series, No. 25. Colorado Springs, Colo., 1962.

————. *Outer Space*. Special Bibliography Series, No. 28. Colorado Springs, Colo., 1963.

U.S. Air University. *USAF Counterinsurgency Orientation Course: Selected Readings*. Maxwell Air Force Base, Ala., 1962.

————. Command and Staff College. *The Free World*. CSC-5. Maxwell Air Force Base, Ala., 1960.

U.S. Arms Control and Disarmament Agency. *A Brief Bibliography: Arms Control & Disarmament*. Publication No. 22. Washington, 1964.

U.S. Army Field Forces, Intelligence Section. *Reading List for Military Intelligence Reserve Officers*. Fort Monroe, Va., 1949.

U.S. Atomic Energy Commission. *Civil Defense against Atomic Warfare: A Selected Reading List*. Prepared for the National Security Resources Board. Washington, 1950.

U.S. Congress, Senate, Committee on Foreign Relations, Subcommittee on Disarmament. *Controlling the Further Development of Nuclear Weapons*. 85th Cong., 2d Sess. Washington, 1958.

U.S. Congress, Senate. *Should Weapons Systems Be Placed under International Control? A Collection of Excerpts and a Bibliography Prepared for the 1964–65 High School Debates*. Library of Congress, Legislative Reference Service, Foreign Affairs Division. Sen. Doc. No. 72, 88th Cong., 2d Sess. Washington, 1964.

U.S. Department of the Army. *Communist China: Ruthless Enemy or Paper Tiger?* Department of the Army Pamphlet No. 20-61. Washington, 1962.

————. *Missiles, Rockets, and Space in War and Peace*. Department of the Army, No. 70-5-6. Washington, 1959.

————. *Soviet Russia: Strategic Survey. A Bibliography*. Department of the Army Pamphlet 20-64. Washington, 1963.

————. *U. S. National Security and the Communist Challenge: The Spectrum of East-West Conflict*. Department of the Army Pamphlet 20-60. Washington, 1961.

————. *U.S. Overseas Bases: Present Status and Future Prospects. A Bibliographic Survey*. Department of the Army Pamphlet 20-63. Washington, 1963.

U.S. Department of the Army, Army Artillery and Missile School, Technical Library. *Bulletin. (New Books Received by USAAMS Technical Library, April-June, 1965.)* Fort Sill, Okla., 1965.

————. *Bulletin. (New Books Received by USAAMS Technical Library, July-August, 1965.)* Fort Sill, Okla., 1965.

————. *Selected Bibliography on Communism.* Fort Sill, Okla., 1965.

U.S. Department of the Army, Army Library. *Disarmament: A Bibliographic Record, 1916–1960.* Prepared by Harry Moskowitz and Jack Roberts, research analysts, Army Library, The Pentagon, at the request of the Office, Special Assistant to the Joint Chiefs of Staff for Disarmament Affairs. Washington, 1960.

————. *Military Aspects of Space Exploration. Special Bibliography* No. 16. Washington, 1958.

————. *U.S. Security, Arms Control, and Disarmament, 1960–1961.* Prepared by Harry Moskowitz and Jack Roberts, research analysts, Army Library, The Pentagon, at the request of the Office of the Secretary of Defense. Washington, 1961.

U.S. Department of State, Division of Library and Reference Services. *Psychological Warfare in Support of Military Operations: A Bibliography of Selected Materials with Annotations.* Bibliography No. 59. Washington, 1951.

U.S. Department of State, Division of Library and Reference Service, Office of Libraries and Intelligence Acquisition. *Intelligence: A Bibliography of Its Functions, Methods, and Techniques.* Distributed by the Office of Intelligence Research. Bibliography No. 33. Washington, 1948.

————. *Intelligence: A Bibliography of Its Functions, Methods, and Techniques. Part II. Periodical and Newspaper Articles.* Distributed by the Office of Intelligence Research. Bibliography No. 33. Washington, 1949.

U.S. Department of State, External Research Staff. *International Affairs: Studies in Progress.* External Research List No. 7.22-1964. Washington, 1964.

U.S. Department of State, Office of Intelligence, Research, and Analysis, External Research Staff. *Soviet Military Doctrine.* External Research Paper No. 141. Washington, 1963.

U.S. Department of State, U.S. Disarmament Administration. *A Basic Bibliography: Disarmament, Arms Control, and National Security.* Department of State Publication No. 7193. Washington, 1961.

U.S. Library of Congress, Reference Department, General Reference and Bibliography Division, Arms Control and Disarmament Bibliography Section. *Arms Control and Disarmament: A Quarterly Bibliography with Abstracts and Annotations.* Vols. I and II. No. 1.

U.S. War Department Library. *National Planning and Strategy: A*

Working Bibliography for the Educational System of Officers of the Army. Washington, 1946.

Where in the World? An Annual Index of War/Peace Information Aids and Services. New York Peace Information Center. New York, 1964.

Williams, Stillman P. *Toward a Genuine World Security System: An Annotated Bibliography for Layman and Scholar.* United World Federalists. Washington, 1964.

World Peace under Law: A Selected Bibliography. Turn toward Peace. New York, 1962.

Wright, Christopher. *Selected Bibliography on Arms Control.* Mimeographed. Council for Atomic Age Studies, Columbia University. New York, 1960. Also published, under title of *Selected Critical Bibliography,* in *Daedalus,* Fall, 1960, pp. 1055–73.

periodical indexes

It was originally planned to examine back files of related periodicals for relevant articles. When the list of periodical titles, however, reached more than eighty, with still more to be added, such an approach became impractical, and it was decided instead to refer to periodical indexes. A total of four were consulted: *Readers Guide to Periodical Literature; Social Science and Humanities Index* (formerly *International Index*); *Public Affairs Information Service Bulletin;* and *Air University Periodical Index.* The first includes most of the popular magazines; the second quite thoroughly covers those in the social sciences; the third is essentially a check, since it includes both areas and is focused on public affairs (it also includes books and papers); the fourth covers military periodicals.

The first three were examined for the years 1946–65 inclusive; the *Air University Periodical Index* did not begin publication until 1948. Listed below are the subject categories in each index consulted.

Readers Guide to Periodical Literature and *Social Science and Humanities Index* (The categories apply to both publications; their format is similar, and both are published by the same company.)

> Anti-missile missiles
> Atomic bombs
> Atomic Development Authority (proposed)
> Atomic power

Atomic warfare
Atomic weapons
Atomic weapons and disarmament
China: armed forces
China: defenses
China: military policy
Deterrence (strategy)
Disarmament
Europe: defenses
Europe, Eastern: defenses
Europe, Western: defenses
France: armed forces
France: defenses
France: military policy
Great Britain: armed forces
Great Britain: defenses
Great Britain: military policy
Guided missile bases
Guided missiles
Hydrogen bomb
Military policy
National defense
North Atlantic Treaty Organization
    Multilateral Force (proposed)
Russia: armed forces
Russia: defenses
Russia: military policy
Strategy
United States: armed forces
United States: defenses
United States: military policy

Public Affairs Information Service Bulletin

Armaments
Atomic bombs
Atomic power

Atomic warfare
Atomic weapons
Ballistic missiles
China: armed forces
China: defenses
China: military policy
France: armed forces
France: defenses
France: military policy
Great Britain: armed forces
Great Britain: defenses
Great Britain: military policy
Guided missile bases
Guided missiles
Military art and science
Military policy
Military power
Military tactics
North Atlantic Treaty Organization
Russia: armed forces
Russia: defenses
Russia: military policy
Satellites, artificial: military applications
Space, outer: military aspects
Space research: military aspects
United States: armed forces
United States: defenses
United States: military policy
War

Air University Periodical Index

Aerospace power
Armed forces: China
Armed forces: Communist bloc
Armed forces: France
Armed forces: free world

Armed forces: Great Britain
Armed forces: NATO
Armed forces: Russia
Armed forces: United States
Atomic bombs
Atomic bombs: tests
Atomic energy
Atomic power
Atomic warfare
Atomic weapons
Attack and defense
Ballistic Missile Early Warning System (BMEWS)
Ballistic missiles
Defense: China
Defense: Europe
Defense: France
Defense: Great Britain
Defense: NATO
Defense: Russia
Defense: United States
Deterrence
Disarmament
Guided missiles
Military art and science
Military bases
Military policy
Military power
Missile defense
Missiles
Naval art and science
North Atlantic Treaty Organization
Nuclear bombs
Nuclear test ban
Nuclear warfare
Nuclear weapons

Sea power
Space warfare
Strategy
Strategy: air
Strategy: naval

This technique made it possible to cover a tremendous number of periodicals relatively efficiently. It seemed a safe assumption that if a periodical was not included in any of the indexes, it was unlikely to be particularly important; relatively few exceptions to this rule were found.

government sources

Even though somewhat tedious, it was not difficult to get lists of published material. Obtaining information on pertinent unpublished papers circulated by institutes, corporations, and universities proved more difficult. Although a few of these were listed in the bibliographies and indexes (especially in *Public Affairs Information Service Bulletin*), it was obvious that they represented only a small part of the available material. In an effort to obtain such information, two techniques were employed. Letters were sent to organizations requesting publication lists (see next section); and since much of this material was prepared for the government under contract, access was gained to a government publication variously entitled *Technical Information Pilot, Title Announcement Bulletin,* and *Technical Abstract Bulletin.* This publication lists papers prepared for the government in the area of defense. It is not complete, but it is a massive piece of reference material.

From 1948 to 1953 it was called *Technical Information Pilot,* and was published by the Science and Technology Project, Library of Congress, for the Office of Naval Research. Categories studied were:

Atomic bomb
Atomic energy
Atomic weapons
Disarmament
Military
Strategy

From 1953 to 1957 it was published as *Title Announcement Bulletin* by the Armed Services Technical Information Agency (ASTIA). Categories studied were:

18 Military science and operations
32 Social science
05 Behavioral science
15 Military

In 1957 the title was again changed, this time to *Technical Abstract Bulletin*. However, both the publishing agency and the categories remained the same, except that the "social science" category was renamed "miscellaneous arts and sciences." It was examined for the years 1958 to 1965 inclusive.

publication lists

Over a period of several months in late 1965 and early 1966, approximately three hundred letters were sent to various institutes and corporations that seemed to have some contact with nuclear strategy and disarmament. The letters explained the purpose of the study and asked for each organization's publication lists, with titles and authors. The results of this inquiry were as follows: twenty-one letters could not be delivered because no satisfactory mailing address could be found; fifty-two were not answered, nor did a follow-up letter bring any result; thirty-three respondents said, or implied, that they had published in the field but were unable, for one reason or another, to send a list of publications; 178 either sent a list or stated that that they had done no work in the field. If the first group is excluded, the "response rate" was 68 percent (*N* was 263). We will consider these groups in reverse order.

The organizations that either sent a publication list or said that they had done no work in the field are listed below. An asterisk (*) indicates that the publication list was not complete (a "complete list" was considered to be one that included the years 1946–65 or beginning with the organization's founding).

Aerospace Industries Association of America, Washington
Air Force Association, Washington
American Academy of Arts and Science, Cambridge, Mass.
American Academy of Political and Social Sciences, Philadelphia*

American Association for the Advancement of Science, Washington

American Bar Association, World Peace through Law Center, Washington

American Chemical Society, New York

American Enterprise Institute for Public Policy Research, Washington

American Ethical Union, New York*

American Foundation for Continuing Education, Aspen, Colo.

American Orthopsychiatric Association, New York

American Peace Terms Committee, Philadelphia

American Security Council, Chicago

American University, Special Operations Research Office, Foreign Areas Studies Division, Washington

Arms Control and Disarmament Agency, Washington*

Army Artillery and Missile School, Fort Sill, Okla.

Army, Department of the, Washington

Army Weapons Command, Rock Island, Ill.

Arthur D. Little Co., Cambridge, Mass.

Association of the United States Army, Washington

Atlantic Research Corporation, Alexandria, Va.

Battelle Memorial Institute, Columbus, Ohio*

Battelle Memorial Institute, Richland, Wash.

Bell Telephone Laboratories, Murray Hill, N.J.*

Bendix Corporation, Bendix Systems Division, Ann Arbor, Mich.

Boston University, Physical Research Laboratories, Boston

Brotherhood of Sleeping Car Porters, New York

Bureau of Social Science Research, Inc., Washington

Burroughs Corporation, Paoli, Pa.*

California Institute of Technology, Jet Propulsion Laboratory, Pasadena, Calif.

Canadian Peace Research Institute, Toronto, Ont.

Carnegie Endowment for International Peace, New York*

Case Institute of Technology, Operations Research Group, Cleveland

Catholic Association for International Peace, Washington, Conn.

Center for the Study of Democratic Institutions, Santa Barbara, Calif.

Central Conference of American Rabbis, New York

Chestnut Lodge Research Institute, Rockville, Md.

Chicago, University of, Center for the Study of American Foreign and Military Policy, Chicago

Colorado State University, Research Foundation, Fort Collins, Colo.

Columbia University, The American Assembly, New York

Columbia University, Bureau of Applied Social Research, New York*

Columbia University, Institute of War and Peace Studies, New York

Columbia University, Russian Institute, New York*

Columbia University, Teachers College, New York

Commission of the Churches on International Affairs, New York

Committee for Economic Development, New York

Conference upon Research and Education in World Government, Chicago

Conservative Society of America, New Orleans*

Cornell University, Center for International Studies, Ithaca, N.Y.

Council for a Livable World, Washington*

Council for a Gradualist Way to Peace, New York*

Council for the Study of Mankind, Santa Monica, Calif.

Council on Religion and International Affairs, New York*

Council on World Tensions, Inc., New York*

Current Affairs Press, New York

Denver University, Denver Research Institute, Denver, Colo.

Denver University, Project DUTY, Department of Geography (Colorado Seminary), Denver, Colo.

Duke University, Rule of Law Research Center, Durham, N.C.

Educational Foundation for Nuclear Science, Chicago

Federal Union, Inc., Washington

Fellowship of Reconciliation, Nyack, N.Y.*

Ford Foundation, New York*

Foreign Policy Association, Inc., New York*

Freedom House, New York

Friends Committee on National Legislation, Washington*

Friends General Conference, Philadelphia

Friends Peace Committee of Philadelphia Yearly Meeting, Philadelphia

Friends World College, East Norwich, N.Y.

General Development Corporation, Elkton, Md.

General Electric Company, Schenectady, N.Y.*

General Electric Company, Technical Military Planning Operation (TEMPO), Santa Barbara, Calif.

George Washington University, Human Resources Research Office, Washington*

Georgetown University, Center for Strategic Studies, Washington

Georgetown University, Institute of World Polity, Washington

Governmental Affairs Institute, Washington

Greater St. Louis Citizens' Committee for Nuclear Information, St. Louis

Greenwich Village Peace Center, New York

Group for the Advancement of Psychiatry, New York

Harvard University, Center for International Affairs, Cambridge, Mass.

Historical Evaluation Research Organization, Washington

Hudson Institute, Harmon-on-Hudson, N.Y.

Hughes Aircraft Company, Fullerton, Calif.*

Hydrospace Research Corporation, Rockville, Md.

Illinois, University of, Institute of Communications Research, Urbana, Ill.*

Industrial College of the Armed Forces, Washington

Institute for American Strategy, Chicago

Institute for Defense Analyses, Arlington, Va.*

Institute for Policy Studies, Washington*

Institute for the Study of National Behavior, Princeton, N.J.

Institute of World Affairs, Inc., New York

International Review Service, New York

Jane Addams Peace Association, Inc., New York

Johns Hopkins University, Washington Center of Foreign Policy Research, Washington

Johnson Foundation, Racine, Wis.

Keynote Publications, New York

Lackland Air Force Base, Personnel Research Laboratory, Aerospace Medical Division, Lackland, Tex.

Lawrence, E. C., Radiation Laboratory, Livermore, Calif.

Lilly Endowment, Inc., Research Program in Christianity and Politics, Indianapolis, Ind.

Lockheed Missiles and Space Corporation, Sunnyvale, Calif.

Lutheran Church in America, Board of Social Ministry, New York

Massachusetts Institute of Technology, Center for International Studies, Cambridge, Mass.

Massachusetts Institute of Technology, Lincoln Laboratories, Lexington, Mass.

Massachusetts Political Action for Peace, Cambridge, Mass.

Mathematica, Inc., Princeton, N.J.*

Methodist Board of Christian Social Concerns, Division of Peace and World Order, Washington

Michigan, University of, Center for Research in Conflict Resolution, Ann Arbor, Mich.*

Michigan, University of, Mental Health Research Institute, Ann Arbor, Mich.

Michigan State University, Department of Communications, East Lansing, Mich.

Midwest Research Institute, Kansas City, Mo.*

Minnesota, University of, Center for International Relations and Arms Studies, Minneapolis, Minn.

Moral Re-Armament, New York

National Bureau of Standards, Washington

National Committee for a Sane Nuclear Policy, Inc., New York*

National Council of American-Soviet Friendship, Inc., New York

National Planning Association, Washington

National Policy Committee, Washington

National Research Council, Washington*

National Research Council on Peace Strategy, New York

Naval Ordinance Test Station, China Lake, Calif.

New World Foundation, New York

New York, State University of, Institute on Man and Science, New York

New York Peace Information Center, New York

Notre Dame, University of, Committee on International Relations, Notre Dame, Ind.

Oklahoma, University of, Research Institute, Norman, Okla.

Peace Research Group, Des Moines, Iowa

Peace Research Laboratory, St. Louis, Mo.

Peace Research Organization Fund, Denver, Colo.

Pendle Hill Pamphlets, Walingford, Pa.

Pennsylvania, University of, Foreign Policy Research Institute, Philadelphia*

Pittsburgh, University of, Pittsburgh

Postwar World Council, New York*

Princeton University, Center of International Studies, Princeton, N.J.*

Promoting Enduring Peace, Ind., Woodmont, Conn.*

Public Affairs Committee, Inc., New York

Public Affairs Institute, Washington*

Quadri-Science, Washington

Radio Liberty Committee, New York*

RAND Corporation,[1] Santa Monica, Calif.*

Rockefeller Brothers Fund, New York

Rockefeller Foundation, New York*

Rutgers University, Eagleton Institute of Politics, New Brunswick, N.J.

San Francisco State College, San Francisco, Calif.

San Francisco State College, Institute for Research on International Behavior, San Francisco*

Sandia Corporation, Albuquerque, N.Mex.

Scientists' Institute for Public Information, New York

Scientists on Survival, Inc., Congress of, New York*

Social Science Research Council, Committee on National Security Policy Research, New York*

Socialist Labor Party, Brooklyn, N.Y.

Society for General Systems Research, Bedford, Mass.

Society for Social Responsibility in Science, Southampton, Pa.

Society for the Prevention of World War III, Inc., New York

South Carolina, University of, Institute of International Studies, Columbia, S.C.

Stanford Research Institute, Menlo Park, Calif.*

Stanford University, Hoover Institution on War, Revolution, and Peace, Stanford, Calif.

Stanford University, Studies in International Conflict and Integration, Stanford, Calif.

---

1. No correspondence was initiated with the RAND Corporation; publication lists available in deposit libraries were used.

Student Peace Union, New York*

System Development Corporation, Santa Monica, Calif.

Turn toward Peace, New York

Twentieth Century Fund, New York

United Presbyterian Church in the United States of America, Board of Christian Education, Office of Church and Society, Philadelphia*

U.S. Air Force Academy, Colorado Springs, Colo.

U.S. Naval Post-Graduate School, Monterey, Calif.

U.S. Naval War College, Newport, R.I.

United World Federalists, Washington*

Universities Committee on Post-War International Problems, Boston

War Control Planners, Inc., Chappaqua, N.Y.

War Resisters League, New York*

Washington University, Committee on Research in International Conflict and Peace, St. Louis, Mo.

Western Behavioral Sciences Institute, La Jolla, Calif.

Westinghouse Atomic Power Department, c/o Westinghouse Education Center, Pittsburgh

Wisconsin, University of, National Security Studies Group, Madison, Wis.

Women's International League for Peace and Freedom, U.S. Section, Philadelphia*

Wright-Patterson Air Force Base, Behavioral Science Laboratory, Dayton, Ohio*

Woodrow Wilson Foundation, Princeton, N.J.*

World Friends Research Center, Philadelphia

World Law Fund, New York

World Peace Foundation, Boston

The institutions that answered but could not send publication lists are named below. The number in parentheses refers to the reason for their refusal, as follows: (1) lists do not exist; they either cannot be compiled or procedure would involve too much work to be possible; (2) lists are restricted because publications were done under government contract.

Acts for Peace, Berkeley, Calif. (1)

Aerospace Corporation, El Segundo, Calif. (2)

American Friends Service Committee, Peace Literature Service, Philadelphia (1)

American Military Institute, Washington (1, apparently)

American University, Special Operations Research Office, Washington (2)

Americans for Democratic Action, Washington (1)

Army, Department of the, Army Library, Washington (1)

Boeing Company, Aerospace Group, Seattle, Wash. (2)

California State College at Los Angeles, Center for the Study of Armament and Disarmament, Los Angeles (1)

Christian Century Foundation, Chicago (1)

Columbia University, Council for Atomic Age Studies, New York (1)

Committee for the Application of the Behavioral Sciences to the Strategies of Peace, San Francisco (1)

Committee for World Development and World Disarmament, New York (1)

Council on Foreign Relations, New York (1)

Federal Procurement Publications, Inc., Long Island, N.Y. (1)

Federation of American Scientists, Washington (1)

Friends Committee on Legislation, San Francisco (1)

Hughes Aircraft Company, Technical Analysis Office, Washington (2)

Human Resources Research Institute, Maxwell Air Force Base, Ala. (1)

ITEK Corporation, Washington (2)

MITRE Corporation, Washington (2)

Ohio State University, Mershon Center for Education in National Security, Columbus, Ohio (1)

Research Analysis Corporation, McLean, Va. (2)

Smithsonian Institution, Washington (1)

State, Department of, Bureau of Intelligence and Research, External Research Staff, Washington (2)

Sylvania Electronic Systems—West, Mountain View, Calif. (2)

Tamiment Institute, Tamiment, Pa. (1)

United Nations Association of the United States of America, New York (1)

United Research, Inc., Cambridge, Mass. (2)

U.S. Naval Institute, Annapolis, Md. (1)

Wright-Patterson Air Force Base, Foreign Technical Division, Air Force Systems Command, Dayton, Ohio (2)

The following institutions did not reply.

Air War College, Maxwell Airforce Base, Ala.

American Peace Society, Washington

American Veterans Committee, Washington

Booz-Allen Applied Research, Bethesda, Md.

California, University of, at Los Angeles, Office of the Coordinator, Overseas Programs, Los Angeles

California, University of, Institute of International Studies, Berkeley

Chicago, University of, Laboratories for Applied Science, Chicago

Colgate University, Atomic Energy Committee, Hamilton, N.Y.

Committee for Non-Violent Action, New York

Congregational Christian Churches, Council for Social Action, New York

CONSAD Research Corporation, Pittsburgh

Consensus on International Affairs, Iowa City, Iowa

Control Data Corporation, Rockville, Md.

Convair, Operations Analysis Group, San Diego, Calif.

Council for Correspondence, Cambridge, Mass.

Creighton University, Center for Peace Research, Omaha, Nebr.

Czechoslovak Institute in Exile, c/o Czechoslovak National Council, Chicago

Defense Research Corporation, Arlington, Va.

Duke University, Research Program in Christianity and Politics, Department of Political Science, Durham, N.C.

Fairleigh Dickinson University, Disarmament Studies Project, Rutherford, N.J.

Foreign Policy Clearing House, Washington

Institute for Arms Control and Peace Research, Ann Arbor, Mich.

International Peace Communications Center, St. Louis, Mo.

League for Industrial Democracy, New York

National Council of the Churches of Christ in the USA, Department of Publications Services, New York

Navy League of the United States, Washington

New Century Publishers, New York

North American Aviation, Inc., Information and Space Systems Division, Downey, Calif.

Northwestern University, Evanston, Ill.

Operations and Policy Research, Inc., Washington

Pacifist Research Bureau, Philadelphia

Peacemakers, Cincinnati, Ohio

Physicians for Social Responsibility, Boston

Pocket Pamphlet Press, Washington

Raytheon Company, Strategic Studies Department, Missile and Space Division, Bedford, Mass.

Social Scientists for Peace, New York

Socialist Workers Party, New York

Society for the Psychological Study of Social Issues, Washington

Society for the Study of Social Problems, International Tensions Committee, Spencer, Ind.

Strategy for Peace Conference, New York

Students for a Democratic Society, New York

Students for a Democratic Society, Boston Peace Research and Education Project, Cambridge, Mass.

Students for a Democratic Society, Peace Research and Education Project, Ann Arbor, Mich.

Technology Planning Center, Inc., Ann Arbor, Mich.

Union Carbide Nuclear Company, c/o Union Carbide, New York

Universities Committee on the Problems of War and Peace, Detroit, Mich.

Utah, University of, Institute of International Studies, Salt Lake City, Utah

Wayne State University, Center for the Teaching about War and Peace, Detroit, Mich.

Western Electric Company, Inc., Industrial Relations Department, South Kearny, N.J.

Whittlesey House, New York

Women Strike for Peace, Washington

World Peace Broadcasting Foundation, Des Moines, Iowa

Letters to the institutions named below could not be delivered by the post office. No doubt many, if not most, of them no longer exist.

Biosophical Institute, New York
Committee for Collective Security, New York
Campaign for World Government, Chicago
Committee for Peaceful Alternatives, New York
Crosscurrents Press, New York
Episcopal League for Social Action, Detroit, Mich.
Greater Chicago Emergency Peace Council, Chicago
In Fact, New York
International Peace Research Institute, Far Hills, N.J.
Methodist Commission on World Peace, Chicago
National Committee on Atomic Information, Washington
National Council for the Prevention of War, Washington
National Council of the Arts, Sciences, and Professions, New York
National Institute of Social Sciences, New York
National Peace Conference, New York
Peace Pamphleteers, Cambridge, Mass.
Southern California, University of, Council on Atomic Implications, Inc., Los Angeles
Systems Research Center, Bedminster, N.J.
Total Peace, Inc., New York
World Events Committee, Washington
World Peace Agency, Chicago

appendix b

mail questionnaire

This appendix contains a copy of the mail questionnaire. All mailings (both original and follow-up) included an appropriate covering letter, a copy of the questionnaire, and a business reply envelope.

Roy E. Licklider

Political Science Research Library

Yale University

89 Trumbull Street • New Haven, Connecticut 06520

1. Name _____

2. Year of birth _____

3. Are you a U.S. citizen?   Yes _____   No _____

4. What college degrees do you hold? (Please do not include honorary degrees.)

       _____ Bachelors
       _____ Masters
       _____ Doctorate (non-medical)
       _____ Doctorate (medical)
       _____ LL.B.
       _____ Other (please specify) _____

5. Please give the following information concerning your *highest* academic degree.

     Degree _____

     Institution _____

     Date _____

     Field of study _____

6. What is (was) your father's occupation? _____

7. Have you ever been employed *full-time* for *over four months* by any of the following types of institutions, doing work that was *directly related to nuclear strategy and disarmament?* (Check as many as are applicable.)

       _____ College or university (teaching full or part time)
       _____ College or university (no teaching responsibility)
       _____ Private, non-profit research and/or educational institute
       _____ Research institute affiliated with a college or university
       _____ Private corporation (not non-profit)
       _____ Periodical (privately owned)
       _____ Federal government
       _____ Other (please specify _____

       _____

8. Have you served in the armed forces? Yes _____   No _____

9. If YES: In what branch did you serve?

       _____ Army   _____ Marines
       _____ Navy   _____ Coast Guard
       _____ Air Force   _____ Other (please specify) _____

10. What was your highest rank? _____

11. About what percentage of your professional time do you *currently* spend in work related to strategy and disarmament?

     _____ 0%–25%   _____ 26%–50%   _____ 51%–75%   _____ 76%–100%   _____ Don't know

12. In the past five years, has this percentage:

     _____ Substantially increased   _____ Not substantially changed   _____ Substantially decreased   _____ Don't know

13. Five years from now, do you expect this percentage to have:
_____ Substantially increased _____ Not substantially changed _____ Substantially decreased _____ Don't know

14. What would you say your profession is? _____

15. To what professional organizations do you belong?
_____
_____
_____

16. Do you consider yourself affiliated with an academic discipline?   Yes ____ No · ____ Don't know ____

   If YES:

   17. What discipline is this? _____

   18. What fields within this discipline have you specialized in, if any?
   _____
   _____
   _____

19. Do you regard yourself as a physical scientist? Yes ____ No ____ Don't know ____

20. Do you regard yourself as a social or behavioral scientist? Yes ____ No ____ Don't know ____

21. Have you ever worked on a government research contract in the area of nuclear strategy and disarmament?

   Yes ____ No _____ Don't know ____

22. Have you ever received a security clearance?   Yes ____ No _____ Don't know ____

23. Several universities are now offering courses in the field of strategy and disarmament. What do you think is the most likely academic future of this field of study?
   ____ Development into a separate discipline
   ____ Development into a recognized interdisciplinary field such as area studies
   ____ Development into a recognized specialty area within a major discipline (what discipline?) _____
   ____ Scattered courses taught by individuals interested in the area in various disciplines
   ____ No courses in the area
   ____ Other (specify) _____
   ____ Don't know

24. Have you ever taught a college course in strategy and disarmament (as distinguished from including sections on this subject within general courses in related areas)?
             Yes ____ No ____ Don't know ____

   25. If NO: Would you like to each such a course?   Yes ____ No ____ Don't know ____

26. Do you expect to teach such a course in the future?   Yes ____ No ____ Don't know ____

27. Do you think that you as an individual have ever significantly influenced a policy of the United States government in the field of strategy and disarmament?
             Yes ____ No ____ Don't know ____

28. How much would you say civilians not employed by the government have influenced American defense policy since World War II?

_____ Not at all   _____ Not very much   _____ Somewhat   _____ A good deal   _____ Very much   _____ Don't know

29. Please indicate opposite each field of study whether you believe that *in the past* its general influence in the area of nuclear strategy and disarmament has been too great, too small, or about right.

	much too great	too great	about right	too small	much too small	don't know
Physical sciences						
Social sciences						
Humanities						
Anthropology						
Area Studies						
Biology						
Chemistry						
Economics						
Engineering						
History						
Law						
Mathematics						
Military and naval science						
Operations research						
Philosophy						
Physics						
Political science						
Psychology						
Sociology						
Theology						

30. Opposite each periodical listed below, please indicate about how often you usually read its articles on the subject of strategy and disarmament.

	Not familiar with periodical	Read only occasional articles	Read less than half the articles on this topic	Read more than half the articles on this topic	Read nearly all the articles on this topic	Don't know
Air Force						
Air University Review ew						
America						
American Historical Review						
American Journal of International Law						
American Political Science Review						
Annals of The American Academy of Political and Social Science						
Army						

30. Opposite each periodical listed below . . . . (Continued)	Not familiar with periodical	Read only occasional articles	Read less than half the articles on this topic	Read more than half the articles on this topic	Read nearly all the articles on this topic	Don't know
Atlantic Monthly	___	___	___	___	___	___
Aviation Week	___	___	___	___	___	___
Bulletin of The Atomic Scientists	___	___	___	___	___	___
Christian Century	___	___	___	___	___	___
Commentary	___	___	___	___	___	___
Commonweal	___	___	___	___	___	___
Current History	___	___	___	___	___	___
Daedalus	___	___	___	___	___	___
Fellowship	___	___	___	___	___	___
Foreign Affairs	___	___	___	___	___	___
Harpers	___	___	___	___	___	___
Intercom	___	___	___	___	___	___
International Conciliation	___	___	___	___	___	___
International Organization	___	___	___	___	___	___
Journal of The Armed Forces	___	___	___	___	___	___
Journal of Conflict Resolution	___	___	___	___	___	___
Marine Corps Gazette	___	___	___	___	___	___
Military Affairs	___	___	___	___	___	___
Military Review	___	___	___	___	___	___
Missiles and Rockets	___	___	___	___	___	___
Nation	___	___	___	___	___	___
National Review	___	___	___	___	___	___
Navy	___	___	___	___	___	___
New Republic	___	___	___	___	___	___
Operations Research	___	___	___	___	___	___
Orbis	___	___	___	___	___	___
Reporter	___	___	___	___	___	___
Saturday Review	___	___	___	___	___	___
Scientific American	___	___	___	___	___	___
Stanford Research Institute Journal	___	___	___	___	___	___
United States Naval Institute Proceedings	___	___	___	___	___	___
Virginia Quarterly Review	___	___	___	___	___	___
War/Peace Report	___	___	___	___	___	___
World Politics	___	___	___	___	___	___
Worldview	___	___	___	___	___	___
Others: _____	___	___	___	___	___	___
_____	___	___	___	___	___	___
_____	___	___	___	___	___	___

31. On the above list, please circle the three periodicals whose articles have been the most influential in your own thinking.

32. Opposite each of the following possible reasons for doing work in the area of strategy and disarmament, please indicate whether it had not much influence, some influence, or very much influence on *your* decision to *enter* the field.

33. Please indicate also whether your *expectations* when you *entered* the field have generally been *fulfilled*.

	Not much	Some	Very much	fulfilled	Not fulfilled	Don't know
a. Desire to significantly alter American foreign policy	___	___	___	___	___	___
b. Concern about the threat of modern weapons to the human race	___	___	___	___	___	___
c. Desire to combat world communism	___	___	___	___	___	___
d. Desire to encourage world disarmament	___	___	___	___	___	___
e. Specific job opportunity	___	___	___	___	___	___
f. Desire to promote democracy throughout the world	___	___	___	___	___	___
g. Desire to teach and disseminate knowledge in this area	___	___	___	___	___	___
h. Intellectual interest in international security affairs	___	___	___	___	___	___
i. Desire to influence young minds	___	___	___	___	___	___
j. Concern about the moral problems of current American military policy	___	___	___	___	___	___
k. Availability of research funds in this field	___	___	___	___	___	___
l. Influence of an individual working in the field	___	___	___	___	___	___
m. Influence of an individual not working in the field	___	___	___	___	___	___
n. Experiences during World War II	___	___	___	___	___	___
o. Related problem in another field	___	___	___	___	___	___
p. Casual exposure to the area	___	___	___	___	___	___
q. Influence of a book or publication in the field	___	___	___	___	___	___
r. College course in the field	___	___	___	___	___	___
s. College course in another field that included a section on this area	___	___	___	___	___	___
t. Other (specify)						
_____	___	___	___	___	___	___
_____	___	___	___	___	___	___
_____	___	___	___	___	___	___
_____	___	___	___	___	___	___

34. In your opinion, what individuals have made the most significant contribution to the study of strategy and disarmament since World War II? After each name, please indicate in a few words the nature of that individual's contribution.

_____

_____

_____

_____

_____

35. What individuals have had the most influence on *your* own thinking and ideas in strategy and disarmament? After each name, please indicate whether this influence was primarily by publications, by personal contact, or both.

_____

_____

_____

_____

_____

36. What problems receive less attention than they should in the field of strategy and disarmament?

_____

_____

_____

_____

37. It has been suggested that there is an "establishment" in the field of strategy and disarmament, a group which sets the limits (perhaps unconsciously) within which strategic debate and discussion is carried on. If you published material of which the "establishment" disapproved, what effects do you think this would have on you?(Check as many as you feel are appropriate.)

____ No effect; there is no "establishment"

____ No effect; the "establishment" has no real power

____ Loss of general respect among colleagues

____ Difficulty in obtaining research funds

____ Difficulty in obtaining good university appointments

____ Not listened to by the government

____ Other (please specify) _____

____ _____

____ _____

____ Don't know

38. How much experience have you had with simulation and gaming techniques? Please check any alternatives that are applicable to you.

____ Totally unfamiliar with the technique

____ Casual knowledge of the technique

____ Have read publications about it

____ Have been involved in one or more simulations

____ Have initiated one or more simulations

____ Have used simulation in making one or more policy decisions

____ Other (please specify) _____

_____

39. Do you think simulation is useful in any of the following areas?

_____ Education   _____ Policy planning

_____ Theory testing   _____ Theory building

_____ Prediction of actual events   _____ Enhancing creativity

_____ Not useful in any way   _____ Don't know

_____ Other (please specify) _____

_____

40. Which of the following do you feel to be strengths and weaknesses of simulation?

	Major strength	Minor strength	Neither strength nor weakness	Minor weakness	Major weakness	Don't know
Abstract nature of simulation	___	___	___	___	___	___
Complexity of simulation	___	___	___	___	___	___
Difficulties of measurement	___	___	___	___	___	___
Use of human decision-makers in some simulations	___	___	___	___	___	___
Failure to use human decision-makers in some computer simulations	___	___	___	___	___	___
Relating simulate time to "real world" time	___	___	___	___	___	___
Other _____	___	___	___	___	___	___
_____	___	___	___	___	___	___
_____	___	___	___	___	___	___

41. Can you imagine any government contract on which you would refuse to work for political or moral reasons? Please check any of the following on which you would refuse to work.

_____ Techniques and utility of preventive war launched by the United States

_____ Establishment of a Doomsday Machine by the U.S.

_____ Unilateral disarmament by the U.S.

_____ Establishment of world government

_____ Techniques for violating an existing arms control agreement by the U.S.

_____ Techniques for violating a prospective agreement on complete and general disarmament by the U.S.

_____ Technique of starting a catalytic war between the Soviet Union and China

_____ Strategy for combating a revolution in the U.S. with nuclear weapons

_____ Techniques for staging a military coup in the U.S.

_____ No government contract would be refused for political or moral reasons

41. Can you imagine any government contract . . . . (Continued)

_____ Other (specify) _____

_____ _____

_____

42. Within the past five years, have you publicly disagreed with a position of the United States government in the area of strategy and disarmament?
_____ Yes   _____ No   _____ Don't know

DO YOU AGREE OR DISAGREE WITH THE FOLLOWING STATEMENTS?

43. Most individuals who have worked in strategy and disarmament since World War II can be classified, without doing too much violence to their positions, as belonging to one of a rather small number of separate groups in terms of their policy positions.

_____ Agree strongly   _____ Disagree strongly

_____ Agree moderately   _____ Disagree moderately

_____ Agree somewhat   _____ Disagree somewhat

_____ Neither agree nor disagree   _____ Don't know

44. Most *organizations* which have done work in strategy and disarmament since World War II can be classified, without doing too much violence to their positions, as belonging to one of a rather small number of separate groups in terms of their policy positions.

_____ Agree strongly   _____ Disagree strongly

_____ Agree moderately   _____ Disagree moderately

_____ Agree somewhat   _____ Disagree somewhat

_____ Neither agree nor disagree   _____ Don't know

45. The study of strategy and disarmament is developing into a new profession.

_____ Agree strongly   _____ Disagree strongly

_____ Agree moderately   _____ Disagree moderately

_____ Agree somewhat   _____ Disagree somewhat

_____ Neither agree nor disagree   _____ Don't know

46. Civilians studying strategy and disarmament have tended to stress technical analysis and to ignore political problems.

_____ Agree strongly   _____ Disagree strongly

_____ Agree moderately   _____ Disagree moderately

_____ Agree somewhat   _____ Disagree somewhat

_____ Neither agree nor disagree   _____ Don't know

47. On the whole, this fact (whether or not civilians have ignored political problems) is a good thing.

_____ Agree strongly   _____ Disagree strongly

_____ Agree moderately   _____ Disagree moderately

_____ Agree somewhat   _____ Disagree somewhat

_____ Neither agree nor disagree   _____ Don't know

48. American foreign policy since World War II has placed too much emphasis on the threat of world communism and the Soviet bloc.

_____ Agree strongly   _____ Disagree strongly

_____ Agree moderately   _____ Disagree moderately

_____ Agree somewhat   _____ Disagree somewhat

_____ Neither agree nor disagree   _____ Don't know

49. Civilians outside of government who are working in the area of strategy and disarmament have been too much concerned with making the present international system more tolerable rather than exploring ways to change the system itself.

_____ Agree strongly   _____ Disagree strongly

_____ Agree moderately   _____ Disagree moderately

_____ Agree somewhat   _____ Disagree somewhat

_____ Neither agree nor disagree   _____ Don't know

50. In ten years China will be a greater threat to the United States than the Soviet Union will be.

_____ Agree strongly   _____ Disagree strongly

_____ Agree moderately   _____ Disagree moderately

_____ Agree somewhat   _____ Disagree somewhat

_____ Neither agree nor disagree   _____ Don't know

51. The present system of deterrance seems unlikely to last until the end of the century without breaking down in a central nuclear war.

_____ Agree strongly   _____ Disagree strongly

_____ Agree moderately   _____ Disagree moderately

_____ Agree somewhat   _____ Disagree somewhat

_____ Neither agree nor disagree   _____ Don't know

52. American foreign policy since World War II has not faced up to the fundamental problem of a hostile Communist foe dedicated to its destruction.

_____ Agree strongly   _____ Disagree strongly

_____ Agree moderately   _____ Disagree moderately

_____ Agree somewhat   _____ Disagree somewhat

_____ Neither agree nor disagree   _____ Don't know

53. It seems likely that, within this century, the Soviet Union and the United States will be allied against China.

    ____ Agree strongly   ____ Disagree strongly

    ____ Agree moderately   ____ Disagree moderately

    ____ Agree somewhat   ____ Disagree somewhat

    ____ Neither agree nor disagree   ____ Don't know

54. The aggressive tendencies of the Soviet Union have been greatly reduced since World War II.

    ____ Agree strongly   ____ Disagree strongly

    ____ Agree moderately   ____ Disagree moderately

    ____ Agree somewhat   ____ Disagree somewhat

    ____ Neither agree nor disagree   ____ Don't know

55. The American policy of containment of the Soviet Union has been a success.

    ____ Agree strongly   ____ Disagree strongly

    ____ Agree moderately   ____ Disagree moderately

    ____ Agree somewhat   ____ Disagree somewhat

    ____ Neither agree nor disagree   ____ Don't know

56. Some form of world government is the only long-term solution to the problem of the destructiveness of modern weapons and opposing nationalisms.

    ____ Agree strongly   ____ Disagree strongly

    ____ Agree moderately   ____ Disagree moderately

    ____ Agree somewhat   ____ Disagree somewhat

    ____ Neither agree nor disagree   ____ Don't know

57. In a nuclear age, the American government must regard itself as being responsible, not only to the American people, but also to the people of the world.

    ____ Agree strongly   ____ Disagree strongly

    ____ Agree moderately   ____ Disagree moderately

    ____ Agree somewhat   ____ Disagree somewhat

    ____ Neither agree nor disagree   ____ Don't know

58. The issues of strategy and disarmament are so complex that it is impossible to conduct meaningful public discussion about them; they are best left to the experts and specialists, under the general guidance of political leaders.

    ____ Agree strongly   ____ Disagree strongly

    ____ Agree moderately   ____ Disagree moderately

    ____ Agree somewhat   ____ Disagree somewhat

    ____ Neither agree nor disagree   ____ Don't know

59. The military should have a greater voice in strategic decisions than it has today.

    ____ Agree strongly   ____ Disagree strongly

    ____ Agree moderately   ____ Disagree moderately

    ____ Agree somewhat   ____ Disagree somewhat

    ____ Neither agree nor disagree   ____ Don't know

60. There is a need for a new professional organization for individuals working in strategy and disarmament.

    ____ Agree strongly   ____ Disagree strongly

    ____ Agree moderately   ____ Disagree moderately

    ____ Agree somewhat   ____ Disagree somewhat

    ____ Neither agree nor disagree   ____ Don't know

61. A researcher has a moral responsibility for the consequences of his work in government policy decisions.

    ____ Agree strongly   ____ Disagree strongly

    ____ Agree moderately   ____ Disagree moderately

    ____ Agree somewhat   ____ Disagree somewhat

    ____ Neither agree nor disagree   ____ Don't know

62. The major threat to American national interests abroad since World War II has been: (choose one)

                     ____ Communist ideology

                     ____ Russian and Chinese national power

63. What is your religion?

    ____ Protestant   ____ Catholic   ____ Jewish   ____ None   ____ Other

64. Please give your current address, if this questionnaire has not been sent there.

    _____

    _____

    _____

    _____

65. I had planned to include a request for a list of your major jobs connected with strategy and disarmament. However, this was discarded as unfair to the respondents because of the work involved. I am interested in obtaining such a list (to study career patterns) if it can be done without troubling you unduly; two obvious sources would be a copy of the appropriate part of your vitae or a reference to any standard biographical work such as *Who's Who In America* or the directory of a professional organization. I would very much appreciate any assistance you can give me in this matter.

                     _____

                     _____

66. If there are any areas that you feel have been inadequately covered or overlooked on this questionnaire, I would appreciate your comments. Thank you very much for your cooperation and for your time.

sample and population

Since the response rate to the mail questionnaire was 39 percent, it was important to determine whether the sample was representative of the population. Two things were known about nearly every member of the population: his publication points score and whether he was a perceived influential as seen by the rest of the sample. Respondents tended to have published somewhat more than nonrespondents; 48 percent of them had scores above 5 (3 was the minimum for inclusion in the population), as compared with 39 percent of the nonrespondents (Ns were 190 and 301, and the difference was statistically significant at the .05 level). Although this difference was statistically significant, it seemed fairly small. Moreover, one criticism of the population criterion was that it included people only marginally interested in the field; this slight skewing of the sample helped to meet this point.

Had the difference really been important, it would presumably have been reflected in the figures concerning perceived influentials. In fact, however, the difference was notable rather than significant; 21 percent of the respondents were perceived influentials, as opposed to 15 percent of the nonrespondents (Ns were 190 and 301 respectively; the significance level was .15).

Obtaining data about nonrespondents was, obviously, somewhat difficult. Given the diverse nature of the population, the standard biographical sources were consulted: *Who's Who in America, Directory of the American Political Science Association, American Men of Science* (both the Physical Science and the Behavioral and Social Science Sections), and *Contemporary Authors;* additional information was gleaned from miscellaneous sources. Information of some sort was thus obtained on 185 (61 percent) of the 301 nonrespondents (one individual sent back

Table 47

INSIGNIFICANT DIFFERENCES BETWEEN RESPONDENTS AND NONRESPONDENTS

	Respondents	Nonrespondents	Significance Level
Highest academic degree			
Bachelor's	25%	25%	
Master's	17	11	
Doctorate	46	47	
Professional	9	9	
No college degree	3	8	.15
School of highest degree			
Ivy League	45	41	
Private, non-Ivy League	26	31	
Public	20	15	
Military	1	2	
Foreign	7	11	NS
Sex			
Male	95	96	NS
Ex-military*	23	28	NS
Branches of Armed Services			
Army	58	49	
Navy	20	24	
Air Force	19	21	
Marine Corps	3	3	
Foreign	0	3	NS

* **Term includes those who had reached rank of captain or lieutenant commander, or higher.**

his questionnaire anonymously; he was thus included twice, as a respondent and a non-respondent). Generally the differences exposed by this information were trivial, as shown in Table 47.

Statistically significant differences appeared in connection with two other variables, but further consideration suggested that neither was as impressive as it first seemed. The difference in religion between respondents and nonrespondents was significant at the .001 level, with nonrespondents much more likely to be Protestant or Catholic rather than Jewish. However, data on this variable were obtained for only 30 of the 301 nonrespondents (about 10 percent). Moreover, as phrased on the questionnaire, the question included a "none" category. It was checked by 34 percent of the respondents, and thus came in a close second to Protestant (37 percent). This category, of course, did not exist in the nonrespondent data. Moreover, religion did not appear to be significant in the analysis. It therefore seems unlikely that the results of this difference are important, although we cannot be completely confident of this.

Table 48

AGE DIFFERENCES BETWEEN
RESPONDENTS AND NONRESPONDENTS

Year of Birth	Respondents	Non-respondents
1880-1899	9%	20%
1900-1919	42	52
1920-1939	48	28
1940-1959	1	0
Total	100	100

Note: Ns were: respondents, 184; nonrespondents, 182. Significance level: .001

A more serious question concerns the age of the respondents and nonrespondents; Table 48 shows that nonrespondents tend to be significantly older (a similar pattern appears in the date of the highest earned academic degree). Although the age variable is not crucial in the analysis, it does play a part. However, data for 68 percent of the nonrespondents came from *Who's Who in America*. It seems likely that individuals who are listed there tend to be older than those who are not, and this may well account for the difference.

One of the more surprising findings of this study concerns the dominance of political scientists.[1] It was thus important to determine whether the respondents had overrepresented political scientists. The evidence is clear. There were four indicators that seemed relevant. The results of Question 16 were used in the analysis of disciplines; it read, "Do you consider yourself affiliated with an academic discipline?" Further questions asked what the discipline was and what fields within it the respondent had specialized in, if any. This information simply was not available in the biographical data on non-respondents.

One alternative was the field of study of the highest earned academic degree. Table 49 shows that, on this indicator, political scientists were indeed overrepresented in the sample, along with history, economics, and the miscellaneous category; this distortion was at the expense of law, religious studies, and physics, and the difference was significant at the .001 level. However, the fact that data were available for only 43 nonrespondents (about 10 percent of the total), lessens confidence in these figures.

A third indicator was question 14: "What would you say your profession is?" Table 50 shows that, once again, political scientists were

Table 49

**FIELD OF STUDY OF HIGHEST EARNED
ACADEMIC DEGREE OF RESPONDENTS AND NONRESPONDENTS**

Field of Study*	Respondents	Non-respondents
Political science	19%	2%
Economics	5	0
History	6	0
Miscellaneous†	5	0
Law	9	30
Religious studies	0	7
Physics	6	16
Other	50	45
Total	100	100

Significance level: .001

* All disciplines are listed where the difference between the two groups is equal to, or larger than, 5 percent.

† Of the nine respondents in this category, four took their degrees in liberal arts, two in liberal arts and sciences, and one each in aeronautics, international organization, and race relations.

1. See chapter 6.

oversampled, and this time a reasonable number of non-respondents were included. However, rather than law, religious studies, and physics, this time the missed people were in journalism and education.

Tables 49 and 50 thus agree that political scientists were over-sampled, but disagree at whose expense this came about (unless sub-stantial numbers of individuals with degrees in law, religious studies, and physics are entering the fields of journalism and education). To confirm this finding, the *Biographical Directory* of the American Poli-tical Science Association (1968 edition) was consulted, and it was found that 27 percent of the respondents were members, whereas only 19 percent of the nonrespondents were (Ns were 190 and 301 respec-tively; the difference was significant at the .05 level). On the basis of this evidence it was concluded that the sample did indeed significantly overrepresent political scientists. Unfortunately, the differences be-tween Tables 49 and 50 make it impossible to determine what groups were underrepresented.

Table 50

PROFESSIONS OF RESPONDENTS AND NONRESPONDENTS

Professions*	Respondents	Non-respondents
Political science	14%	1%
Miscellaneous†	8	0
Journalism	9	25
Education	1	12
Other	76	63
Total	100	100

Note: Ns were: respondents, 181; nonrespondents, 159. Significance level: .001

* All categories are included in which the difference between the two groups was equal to, or larger than, 5 percent.

† Of the fourteen respondents in this category, nine were involved with either management or administration, two were consultants, and one each was a foundation staff member, po-litical analyst, and public speaker.

The difference is not unimportant. Chapter 6 is concerned with the differences between members of different academic disciplines, and it does suggest that there are a few—especially in periodicals read and motives for working in the field. (Certain tables in the chapter were corrected to allow for this overrepresentation of political scientists.) However, the differences were not large and seemed to hold only in certain particular areas.

The question of whether any sample is "sufficiently" representative cannot be given a single answer; each individual must make up his own mind about how much he is prepared to rely on it. It was concluded that the only major problem with this sample was that it had too large a proportion of political scientists, but that this was not a major barrier to its use. The above data are presented here so that each reader may reach his own conclusions.

index